Beyond Beauty

Beyond Beauty

By Federico Vercellone
Translated by Sarah De Sanctis

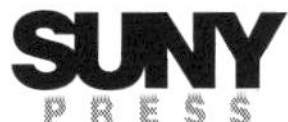

Questo libro e' stato realizzato anche grazie ad un contributo
alla traduzione assegnato dal Ministero degli Affari Esteri
e della Cooperazione Internazionale Italiano

This book has been published also thanks to a translation grant given by the Italian
Ministry of Foreign Affairs and International Cooperation.

Oltre la bellezza ©2008 by Società editrice il Mulino, Bologna

Published by State University of New York Press, Albany

© 2017 Sarah De Sanctis

For information, contact State University of New York Press, Albany, NY
www.sunypress.edu

Production, Jenn Bennett
Marketing, Michael Campochiaro

Library of Congress Cataloging-in-Publication Data

Names: Vercellone, Federico, author.
Title: Beyond beauty / by Federico Vercellone ; translated by Sarah De Sanctis.
Other titles: Oltre la bellezza. English
Description: Albany : State University of New York, 2017. | Series: SUNY series in
    contemporary Italian philosophy | Includes bibliographical references and index.
Identifiers: LCCN 2016037238 (print) | LCCN 2016042264 (ebook) | ISBN
    9781438465876 (hardcover : alk. paper) | 9781438465883 (pbk : alk paper) |
    ISBN 9781438465890 (e-book)
Subjects: LCSH: Aesthetics, Modern—20th century.
Classification: LCC BH204 .V4713 2017 (print) | LCC BH204 (ebook) |
    DDC 701/.17—dc23
LC record available at https://lccn.loc.gov/2016037238

10 9 8 7 6 5 4 3 2 1

Contents

Preface

This book appeared in Italy in 2008. Since then, the reflection and debate on the relationship between beauty and the twentieth century has greatly widened. Many more texts have dealt both with the overall theme of beauty and the more specific theme "beauty and the twentieth century." However, despite the fact that the bibliography on the matter has become much vaster, I believe the fundamental thesis of my book can stay essentially unchanged. If the twentieth century was by vocation devoted to ugliness and the most decisive negation of beauty, it did so not because it denied the significance and necessity of beauty, but rather because beauty appears as a kind of unattainable ideal that nevertheless is eventually bound to come back to the steep and rough terrain of this world to find its proper place. In this way the twentieth century actually played along with the originary vocation of beauty as it was identified in particular by classic German aesthetics: the reappropriation of ethos.

This is the framework of the relation between beauty and twentieth century as it appears in the present book: it starts early and paradoxically with the Frühromantik, passing through Nietzsche and Spengler, Benedetto Croce's aesthetics, the conflicting relationship between Adorno and Heidegger, and finally coming—through surrealism, Barnett Newman, Pollock, and Duchamp—to Andy Warhol's pop art. In line with Arthur Danto's thesis, in this context Warhol appears as a sort of landing point of beauty, which has returned to the world after having discredited and exhausted, through a long erosive process, the roots of its idealization.

All this is concomitant with the exhaustion of the very raison d'être of philosophical aesthetics understood as a discipline that, also based on the idealization of beauty, legislates and takes a regulatory approach to art. On the other hand, contemporary art, and especially conceptual art, decidedly claims the autonomy of its expressive and semantic means, rejecting any form of subjection to philosophical speculation. The traditional prerogatives of the philosophy of art, its categories and its canons are now seen as intrusive, arrogant, and almost devoid of any intimate legitimacy to orient art to its own self-understanding. This paves the way to a very ambivalent situation in which not only the prerogatives but the very scope of action of aesthetics as philosophy of art are questioned while, at the same time, a sort of opaque zone or dark forest appears in which the criteria of judgment on art, delegated exclusively to art itself, end up becoming self-referential and prey of the "art institution," which imposes itself with an attitude of sovereign independence that—ironically and almost unabashedly—is only affected by the market.

In this framework in which autonomous art and the philosophy of art see their traditional spaces and their age-old and often contentious partnership vanish, there seems to be no other chance than that to rehabilitate ethos. In other words, the only solution is to do what the twentieth century has tried to do: give beauty back to the world.

Acknowledgments

I am very grateful to all those who have helped me write this book with their advice, suggestions, and objections. I owe a lot to Claudio Ciancio, who has read the manuscript in its several drafts and never failed to give me precious and friendly advice. Many thanks also to Sergio Givone for following this work in all its (sometimes tiring) phases. I express my gratitude to Mauro Bozzetti, Flavio Fergonzi, Gianluca Garelli, Chiara Giuntini, Maria Passaro, and Enrica Villari for their valuable suggestions. Thanks to Olaf Breidbach and Angelo Vianello for the view of nature that emerges in these pages even when I speak of art. Finally, I am particularly grateful to Laura Anna Macor, who helped me in the final stage of this work.

Beauty and the Twentieth Century

Les plus riches cités, les plus beaux paysages,
Jamais ne contenaient l'attrait mystérieux
De ceux que le hasard fait avec les nuages.
Baudelaire, Le Voyage

Does Beauty Have a History?

Let's be honest: there hasn't been much beauty in the twentieth century—rather, that period fully experienced its absence. There are no characters in flesh and bone here: this is a ghost story, and the protagonist is the spectre of beauty.

Also, the issue is really complex. When one speaks of beauty and the twentieth century, in fact, one is juxtaposing two notions that seem rather distant: an idea—something such as beauty, which tends to the absolute—is set next to a century—that is, a historical determination. This step already shows the terms of a crisis that presents itself almost as a conflict between the two elements: a sort of sharp contrast that has been noted more than once.[1]

Thus, many questions are raised from the very beginning: Does the twentieth century have its own ideal of beauty? Or was it instead a time of violent friction with beauty, a time that no longer wanted to contemplate it or enclose it in the cosmos of its values? Besides, often it was the artists themselves who seemed to have chosen this direction. In this respect, Barnett Newman made a very famous statement in 1948, at the peak of abstract expressionism: "The impulse of modern art is this desire to destroy beauty."[2] So, are we dealing with a sober century, one that has no interest in beauty and chooses functionality and utility instead? Some thought beauty would have been an inappropriate expression on the world's troubled face "after Auschwitz"—Is this what Theodor Wiesengrund Adorno exemplarily testifies to?

In any case, however you want to frame the issue, the very formulation "Beauty and the Twentieth Century" raises a lot of problems. Most of all, they concern the very structure of the phrase. In fact, regardless of the meaning or scope one attributes to the historical context of reference, saying "Beauty *and* the Twentieth Century" means joining an atemporal ideal to a historical climate. Therefore the title shows a contradiction, an impossibility, if you like, that marks the book in its entirety. However, at least we have taken a first step: we have acknowledged the intrinsically contradictory nature of the problem, which will allow us not to be surprised when we come across its torn and suffering face.

Hence a second issue, the following: in principle, or at least with regards to its claims (which we see shortly), beauty does not have a history. Nevertheless, there is a history of the concept of beauty that exposes its varying a-temporal aspirations. Once again we can find a contradiction here, albeit less evident and sharp than the former. We are dealing with an objective multiplication of the models of beauty. Are there many "beauties"? Are we falling into historical relativism?

Not yet. In fact, it is not obvious that those who admit the varied face of the ideal of beauty should speak of it in the plural. In the great age of the metaphysics of beauty, from the ancient times to the eighteenth century, the issue appeared differently. It concerned the borders and configuration of beauty: those who came before, according to their successors, were unable to offer an adequate description of the idea, which should therefore be 'adequately' rewritten.

Now, things are very different if one wants to give a 'better' description of the characteristics of beauty or if, on the contrary, one claims that beauty cosubstantially belongs to history, as has happened since the nineteenth century. This completely revolutionized the terms of the issue and produced a crisis of beauty as an ideal. As we see, this coincided with the fact that beauty, from then on, had to recognize itself in a diminished form, and only in the guise of art. This is the limit, but also the beginning of our story, which is enclosed here under the title "Beauty and the Twentieth Century."

A History of Beauty

The history of beauty, for a great part, does not at all coincide with that of the fine arts. At first, and for a very long time, the destiny of beauty was not connected to art but to nature and, in particular, to living beings. In ancient times beauty came to take on a moral meaning, and this was gradually lost in the path of culture, while being still strongly felt by common sense even today. In fact, we still use the term "beautiful" not only with regards to real people, but also to behaviors that we are assessing from a moral standpoint—for instance, a beautiful gesture.

At the origins of philosophy, with the Pythagoreans—thanks to what was defined "the Great Theory"[3]—beauty asserts a substantial harmony that primarily concerns the cosmos. It notes a surprising regularity of nature that, in all likelihood, also implies the possibility—which appeared in myth even before philosophy—that the latter can be dominated.[4] It reveals an 'objective' intelligence, inherent in living forms and in their regularity.

Besides, this early philosophical systematization brings out a powerful aspect of the original myth announcing the rise of beauty: the myth recounted by Hesiod in his *Theogony*, narrating Aphrodite's birth from the water. It expresses the possibility that there should be order beyond the original chaos, that there should be a form able to overcome its magmatic origin. It also expresses the very possibility that being, in its "terrible" contingency, should be able to distance itself from nothingness. Thus, beauty is much more than itself (as it is in modern ages): it transcends the world of appearance and art and contemplates all that exists, especially the order inherent to it, thus being close to truth.

Hesiod's myth recounts that Aphrodite was born from the violent end of the incestuous embrace between Uranus and Gaia, by the hand of Cronos. The union of Heaven and Earth literally swallowed everything within itself. This myth says it all about the odyssey of the form, and how hard it was for being to emerge out of a conflicting and chaotic background. Despite the positive ending, the mythical scene is rather crude at the beginning: urged by his mother, Cronos emasculates his father, Heaven, whose drops of semen fall into the sea and turn into sea foam. Hence—the birth of Aphrodite, who arrives first at Cytherea and then in Cyprus.

Aphrodite thus stands out as an event, as the successful outcome of a cruel conflict, as the generation of order starting from initial chaos.[5] And chaotic also means bad, threatening, something that—just like monsters of all ages—cannot let us see the bottom of its being. Thus beauty, embodied by Aphrodite, represents much more than what today we would call an "aesthetic predicate": her birth allows for the powerful regularity of being—powerful insofar as it makes the latter observable and transparent. In this sense, it is not a false appearance but a manifestation of the truth. And this power is revealed in the image and through it. This is why the visual arts are the real focus of this book.

In this way, mythical image immediately is also somewhat a project or, rather, a semiproject: while describing reality it actually anticipates it, it stands before it, referring to the habitability of the cosmos asserted by its regular, harmonic, and eurhythmic nature. Thus beauty, born in Greece in the name of contemplation, actually presents its ecstatic face in conjunction with a "technological" aspect, one that developed in the post-Platonic tradition especially with Aristotle and his attention to the different forms of artistic *poiesis*.[6] It predisposes the human settlement in the world.

All of this found a conceptual affirmation in the Pythagorean theory, for which order and proportion are not only beautiful but also useful, whereas the opposite can be said of disorder and imbalance. Harmony, symmetry, eurhythmy refer precisely to the measure, the commensurability of the cosmos, which is then recognized as finite.[7] The measure that is intrinsic to beauty and to the cosmos that represents it, also refers to a latent but fundamental, broadly ecological element: the habitability of this very cosmos, which is made such—a kind of huge megaentity complete in itself—thanks to beauty. Insofar as it is endowed with order and measure—therefore, insofar as it is not a chaotic (and therefore potentially aggressive) magma, the cosmos is inhabitable and allows for human settlement.

Moving on to Platonic thought, we find ourselves before the great metaphysical spectacle offered by the ontology of beauty—a beauty that pervades the cosmos as a whole and has nothing to do—at least at first—with art. Thus in Plato, the idea of beauty as an event, which had affirmed itself at the origin of Hesiod's myth, fades. Its project-like nature, along with its evenemential character, pales in front of the superb metaphysical structures that fit deontological description better than history. Nevertheless, description might actually aim at stabilizing what happens and give it the yearned-for regularity. The very fact that the cosmos is alive—as emerges in Plato's work and in particular in *Timaeus*, where the Pythagorean influence is felt the most—is related to its beauty insofar as its components are articulated in a balanced and, therefore, perfect way.

Thus, beauty is akin to good and therefore to the moral sphere, according to a trend we find not only in ancient times but also in the Middle Ages. Once again, this has nothing to do with its modern perception in the isolated sphere of aesthetics. In a way, beauty refers to the model of the living body: the articulation is beautiful insofar as it reveals itself in the part/whole interaction typical of an organism. Once again, we find this view in *Timaeus*, where the cosmos is described as "a Living Creature endowed with soul and reason" resembling "that intelligible Creature which is fairest of all and in all ways most perfect"—an immense organism regulated by number relations in the interrelation of its parts.[8]

On the other hand, this idea of beauty as cosmic and organic perfection—which makes itself heard again between Kant and Romanticism—goes hand in hand with a strictly metaphysical approach, or rather an ontological one, for which (as *Hippias Major* testifies) the definition of beauty cannot be drawn from single examples but must come from the definition of its essence. Exemplification, as such, cannot exhaust the landscape of beauty. Thus the question about the being of supreme evidence precedes every positive instance of it—and it is hard not to note the paradox here. Socrates ironically asks himself: "Come Socrates, answer me. All these things which you say are beautiful, if the absolute beautiful is anything, would be beautiful?"[9]

Besides, Plato's very condemnation of art as it appears in book 10 of the *Republic* can be read only as its defeat in the conflict with beauty, which refers to much higher models. Art reflects an order that does not belong to it originally: this is what Plato's accusation is based on. This is a passage of great significance, in which art takes the status that common sense still attributes to it today: that of appearance. Art imitates what exists, which in turn is nothing but a copy of what truly is: "'Consider, then, this very point. To which is painting directed in every case, to the imitation of reality as it is—or of appearance as it appears? Is it an imitation of a phantasm or of the truth?' 'Of a phantasm,' he said.'"[10]

If in *Republic* art takes on the status of appearance—a status that modern tradition gives it permanently—it is because it is a pale reflection of the metaphysical order for which it can speak only weakly. Thus begins Platonism in art—a change of paradigm so important that it largely coincides with the birth of aesthetics and its development up to what it is today. At that point philosophy affirmed the truth of art, while in modern times art tends to reject this role. Even though the relationship between art and truth has changed over time—at least until the twentieth century when art became the bearer of philosophical truth—things haven't changed too much: art was always legitimated by philosophy, which (ever since Romanticism) led to sharp conflicts and to art's hyperbolic claim of its own autonomous truth.

This story, which lasted many centuries, started with Plato's contraposition between art and beauty and ended only in the twentieth century, when the bond of mutual anagnorisis between art and philosophy (or rather, art's demand for truth from philosophy and the latter's refusal) was broken. This bond was so important that one could define it as foundational for the history of aesthetics. On these grounds philosophy regulates the truth of art and defines its boundaries and competences. If the cons of this situation of subjection are evident right from the start, the pros— as you see[11]—are revealed only later, at the end of the story.

To go back to Plato and the Platonic tradition, beauty is therefore much more than itself: it involves a wide sphere of which it actually represents the measure, becoming, on this basis, the image of goodness. Thus beauty is preparing to make its entrance among the first principles of being, as is certified in medieval philosophy, which sometimes sets it alongside three other transcendentals: *unum, verum, bonum.*[12]

In any case, even taking on a metaphysical-descriptive structure, beauty never denies the broadly project-like character that myth and the related imagery have assigned to it. The project-like side is rather progressively disguised as description. The 'so and so' of metaphysical description does not merely indicate how things are, but also states that they should be such: in other words, it introduces prescription into description. From this point of view, moreover, it is also possible to grasp a surprising continuity in the history of aesthetics that goes from ancient times to today, from the Pythagoreans to the eighteenth-nineteenth century philosophy of art. Beauty, setting itself as a parameter-goal of being, from this perspective, tends to produce itself as art (which is a paradox one must note and not forget).

Late ancient times and the Middle Ages are strongly influenced by Platonism, which still echoes in neo-Platonism. The issue is very significant because it is through Plotinus's—and mostly through Pseudo-Dionysius's—mediation that the Platonic tradition reaches the Middle Ages. This is a secret "morphological revolution": the idea of beauty changes and, most of all, becomes simpler. From the idea of an articulated cosmos we come to the idea of a simple and supreme entity to which beauty alludes. Thanks to this change, beauty can now enter the Christian cosmos and take a path across the Middle Ages and the Renaissance that I cannot address here. I'll merely highlight the long-lasting importance of the Pythagorean system taken up by Platonism: in the light of this, beauty persists as the ideal of a measure and an order that one sees in reality (even though, perhaps, it is rather a wish) and, in various occasions, it is set next to the other transcendentals. Only on a secondary level does beauty concern art.

It is only with Winckelmann that ideal beauty—coinciding with the historical age of ancient Greece—also appears as art; it is only with Kant that there will be an "aesthetic" reading of beauty that (without being yet confined to the domain of art) ends up being (programmatically) deprived of its ancient power. According to the first phase of the *Judgment of Taste*, "the beautiful is that which [. . .] is represented as the object of a universal satisfaction" and "the satisfaction which determines the judgement of taste is disinterested." The *aesthetica* are being turned into *anaesthetica*:[13] what makes beauty attractive must be suppressed; every temptation to consume it must be excluded, so that it can have universal value. With the birth of aesthetic consciousness, beauty becomes both a repertoire and a landscape. It is aesthetic imaginary itself that founds its best-fitting institution: the museum.[14]

In the meantime—and also thanks to this change—the definitive transformation of aesthetics into philosophy of art is taking place: aesthetics has gradually become an autonomous discipline, devoted to perception or sensible knowledge. Thus beauty, devoid of power and any sensible attractive features, ends up closed off in its own sphere, increasingly further away from nature (which Kant was aware of). Beauty, so to speak, is 'made captive': it has been taken hostage by aesthetic thinking. The immense power of beauty, which used to be the appropriate image of the *ordo universalis*, fades away.

Beauty, which has lost its *ubi consistam*, is now also the object of desire: the ultimate goal of a utopian anagnorisis reverberating with beauty's old project-like nature, which was always hidden behind its descriptive trait. That's how the controversial writer of the so-called *Systemprogramm*, the first draft of a system of German idealism, can argue in favor of the future relevance of beauty, reminding the reader that it is the idea that "comprises all ideas" because "*truth and goodness* are united like sisters *only in beauty*."[15]

Transformed into a utopian ideal, beauty appears as the painful symptom of an absence, and the void it has left is occupied by the ugly. This is what young Friedrich Schlegel brilliantly notes in an essay that, perhaps not coincidentally, is coeval of *Systemprogramm*, entitled "On the Study of Greek Poetry." Schlegel could not be clearer. The beautiful has gone missing and the ugly has taken its place:

> Every principle [. . .] except that of *beauty*. This is to such an extent not the governing principle of modern poetry that many of its most splendid works are openly representations of the *ugly*. One must finally, if reluctantly, admit that there does indeed exist a representation of

confusion in all its plentitude, of despair characterized by boundless vigor, that demands an equal if not greater creative power and artistic wisdom than is required from the representation of abundance and vigor in complete harmony. The most praised modern poems appear to be different from this type of art more in degree than manner. If a faint hint of perfect beauty is found, it is experienced not so much in serene enjoyment as in *unsatisfied longing*. The more vigorously one strives after it, the more one distances oneself from the beautiful. The *boundaries* of science and art, of the true and the beautiful, are so confused that even the conviction that those eternal boundaries are permanent has generally begun to falter for the most part. Philosophy poeticizes and poetry philosophizes: history is treated as poetry and poetry is treated as history. Even the types of poetry exchange their very definition. A lyrical mood becomes the object of a drama, and dramatic material is forced into lyrical form. This *anarchy* is not confined to the outer limits; rather, it spans the entire realm of taste and art.[16]

For Schlegel, it is precisely by sinking into the abyss, in the heart of this energetic dissolution of modern art, that beauty shines like the North Star from an infinite distance, in its ancient countenance of something close to the truth and—one may well assume—even to goodness.

In Myth, Beyond Myth

It is not accidental but rather programmatic that, soon after, the philosophy of art was born with Hegel. In his *Aesthetics: Lectures on Fine Art*, he states that the latter can be identified neither with the theory of sensible knowledge, as had happened in the eighteenth century, nor with the theory of beauty, but rather with the "philosophy of art," or better, with the "philosophy of beautiful art."[17] Thus nature, which had been beauty's primary object of attention, is definitely and programmatically pushed into the background in favor of artistic beauty. Hegel says about it:

> In ordinary life we are of course accustomed to speak of a *beautiful* colour, a *beautiful* sky, a *beautiful* river; likewise of *beautiful* flowers, *beautiful* animals, and even more of *beautiful* people. We will not here enter upon the controversy about how far the attribute of beauty

is justifiably ascribed to these and the like, and how far, in general, natural beauty may be put alongside the beauty of art. But we may assert against this view, even at this stage, that the beauty of art is higher than nature. The beauty of art is beauty *born of the spirit and born again*, and the higher the spirit and its productions stand above nature and its phenomena, the higher too is the beauty of art above that of nature. Indeed, considered *formally* [i.e., no matter what it says], even a useless notion that enters a man's head is higher than any product of nature, because in such a notion spirituality and freedom are always present. Of course, considered in its content, the sun, for example, appears as an *absolutely necessary* factor [in the universe] while a false notion vanishes as *accidental* and transitory. But, taken by itself, a natural existent like the sun is indifferent, not free and self-conscious in itself; and if we treat it in its necessary connection with other things, then we are not treating it by itself, and therefore not as beautiful.[18]

Thus art came to definitively replace nature in the hierarchies of beauty. This was an incredibly significant change of paradigm, one in which nature was aesthetically coagulated into the shapeless and chaotic dimension of the sublime—as we see especially in Romantic aesthetics—while beauty loses its quality of "measure of being." Thus we reach an unequivocal and almost definitive crisis of beauty, which has lost its main orientation point and—taking shape almost exclusively in art—ends up falling into intimate self-contradiction. Hence the abovementioned paradox for which beauty, the measure par excellence, constructs itself.

The "technical" face of beauty that already appeared in Hesiod's myth, for which it is both (manifestly) measure and (latently) project, comes here to the final goal of its journey. Now beauty is endowed almost definitively with a technical-constructive aspect: it has become an artwork and, being embodied by an artifact, it builds itself, too. Measure thus—both paradoxically and nihilistically—becomes measure of itself. And this has fatal consequences. The artwork run through by the Hegelian negative shows that classical beauty—the aesthetic measurement par excellence—is not timeless, but the outcome of a process. In this way the balance of beauty turns out to be precarious and produces its own overcoming.[19]

For Hegel, all of this causes the contemporary end of art (at least "considered in its highest vocation") and, at the same time, of beauty. Almost as a compensation for this initial failure, aesthetic thinking and the consciousness accompanying it are exhaustively defined. What is being witnessed—of which Hegel writes so eloquently—is an extraordinary work of condensation of the universe of the image in the sign of aestheticization and, therefore, of appearance, or better, of fiction. It is an enormous work of depowering, so to speak, of 'enclosure' of the lands of imagination that, in the name of art, fall into the category of ineffectuality. The ancient power of the image is thus fully demeaned: it is now banned from any real fact, which is left to mythical narration.

The Spectre of Beauty

Here finally begins our story, which, in many ways, truly is a ghost story. Everything happens *post hoc*: people rush to the deathbed of beauty when it's too late. But even if this ghost is rarely reincarnated, in the twentieth century beauty constitutes a very significant presence/absence.[20] Sure, in the final phase of its history it was emptied of any content or attractive feature and was gradually reduced to becoming nothing but "a promise of happiness."[21] And yet in the twentieth century this promise has great fascination and a specific status. It looms with all the power of those who are not there—its status is mainly evocative. In the past century, the problem of beauty as an aesthetic form that is both measure and principle of being comes back to the fore in many disguises, which must be identified in their historical development and, mostly, in their conceptual traits.

The crisis of beauty in the twentieth century—which was then fully acquired and almost taken for granted—reveals itself as a crisis of the aesthetic intelligence of form (which has always competed with the conceptual one) that accompanies the acclaimed crisis of the intelligibility of the art object. As always, the problem does not concern only art or the arts that, in the meantime, have become "no longer fine."[22] The main character of the twentieth century is that art becomes aware of its inadequacy to express beauty. But what mostly comes out is the reaction to this setback: the fact that art, despite everything, wants to be vicarious for the absent beauty. Which, in the end, it will be.

This is extremely interesting because, in this very way, the ancient status of beauty comes back. The nineteenth century still runs after beauty and tries to appropriate it, sometimes embodying explicitly aesthetic ideals—think of the dandy.[23] The twentieth century, instead, seems to have a mourning and, at the same time, evocative attitude towards beauty: it addresses something that is not (no longer) there and that can be observed from a great distance, as if it were a memory or the yearned-for place of an impossible anagnorisis. If one really wants to realize it in the terms of tradition, one inevitably falls into the *kitsch*—as demonstrated by Hermann Broch.[24] Thus beauty, in its paradoxical existence *in absentia*, goes back to its ancient metaphysical status. Its definitive disappearance, also from the aesthetic scene, paradoxically refers to that 'beyond' (much more than artistic) that only beauty can intrinsically point at.

The answer to this crisis is basically a sort of sublime push of the contemporary artwork, aspiring to realize the unity that, in the meantime, has gone missing. It is in the attempt to overcome this setback that one sees the concretization of the decisive impetus: that towards an anagnorisis (impossible in life) that pervades the avant-garde.[25] The latter is the artistic phenomenon that, in its successive waves, is the real icon of the twentieth century. Following the fleeting imperative of modernity and constantly chasing the new, the form of avant-garde alludes to something that lies beyond itself—it looms as an unfinished form, incomplete, yet always on the way to identify itself with some content that transcends it.[26]

It is the supreme principle of order and legitimacy: the spirit of absent beauty. Moreover, when beauty wants to appear again in the twentieth century as a living presence—that is, if it wants to return under the guise of classicism, it cannot help displaying a rigid mortuary fixity and claiming to establish an order that also holds for social life (think of the art of totalitarian regimes): a normativity whose justness is unconvincing, whilst being strongly coercive.

The awareness that form was no longer able to provide a principle of measure—and therefore of knowledge—had already been spreading in the late nineteenth century and early decades of the twentieth century. Such a journey begins with a great, often overlooked, author: Oswald Spengler. In him one can see the peak of the tension and crisis of the form as an aesthetic principle of knowledge. The ancient morphological knowledge shows its final splendor in a great and utterly questionable text that explicitly, deliberately, is placed at the end of an era (attested by the end of World War I): *The Decline of the West*. For the last time here, the idea of form understood (à la Goethe) as *analogon* of beauty—that is, as a complex system able to gather and realize the complexity of reality in the contemporaneity of the intuited given—proposes itself as the active center of a culture and its self-understanding. In this frame, form is not an element but a complex system: it produces an aesthetic system of correspondences of which art is one of the many components. Every element refers to another, in an interplay of infinite analogical allusions.

The decline of morphology—the type of knowledge that had always been inherent in beauty—also led even further towards a decided aesthetic nominalism. The centrifugal forces of modernity are by now exorbitant;[27] its works have lost any canonical and definitive reference point, from the supreme norm of beauty to the partition of artistic and literary genres. . . . It is as if, from a certain point onwards, we were dealing with a solitary form, devoid of orientation, which does not contain, which loses its ability to aggregate and to realize the complexity in itself, which cannot hold on to the content that it used to be able to express.

The rise of avant-garde—as German expressionism shows exemplarily—also produces a movement of spiritualization of the form that no longer aims at real, mimetically reproducible contents; it no longer aims at representation, the ancient, now lost *pendant* of the metaphysical principle. The system of correspondences guaranteeing the solidity of the entire metaphysical building has crumbled. Thus form seeks one last impossible anagnorisis by turning to infinity, while reality escapes the sphere of aesthetic representation and becomes more singular and objective: more and more (only) itself.

According to Ernst Bloch in his *Spirit of Utopia,* German expressionism is a "metaphysically eidetic" art, an heir of Gothic art, more devoted to the idea than its sensible concretization: an art that is expressed on the path towards an "irreversible eruption of [. . .] mystical nominalism."[28] Then, after Bloch and neo-Marxism, there is Croce, who sets aside all aesthetic categories and focuses exclusively on the artwork—which, paradoxically, contradictorily realizes the supreme invariant: beauty. This paves the way to the end of the concept of artwork, now devoid of any correspondence in a transcendent system, as we see shortly.

The paradox of Croce's solution, which annihilates any distance between the two moments, shows the unbearable tension that now pervades the relationship between art and beauty (mirroring the ancient Platonic relation between philosophy and art). The oppositional relationship between the two terms of the comparison is destined to reach the point of maximum tension, until art decides to assert its rights against philosophy. Beauty evoked from afar is suddenly denied—even more radically than by philosophy—by the philosophical claim that art be the bearer of an autonomous truth, which does not depend on the bounds of philosophy. The history of beauty seems to come here to a sudden end.

This is what can be drawn from the conflicting views expressed at a distance by Martin Heidegger and Theodor Wiesengrund Adorno, where the relation between art and philosophy is taken to its extreme limits in an unequalled confrontation; in it, Adorno fights one more time for the right of philosophy—and therefore of beauty—over art. In this frame, for Adorno, precisely insofar as it is recognized in its ancient majesty, beauty cannot rule the world and therefore art—if it did, it would betray its status and recognize in reality the order that beauty, in its contiguity with other transcendentals, claims to define as true and just. From this point of view, Adorno gives voice in the most extreme and rigorous way to what we call "twentieth century."

As for Heidegger, we can witness something completely opposite. In Heidegger—as testified in particular by the essay on "The Origin of the Work of Art"—it is art, as opposed to philosophy, that takes back its truth, regardless of beauty. In this way, however, it is art itself that becomes a bearer of philosophical truth, leading to a territory that takes aesthetic nominalism to its extreme consequence (and, at the same time, paves the way to the aestheticization of philosophy). Every artwork, embodying truth, is much more than itself. It is all art at once and its truth, or better: truth *tout court*. Thus, even the last aesthetic invariant comes to an end: the unity, the microcosmos represented by the notion of 'artwork,' which could exist only in the distant conceptual relation with the macrocosmos of beauty, ceases to exist.

Thus we witness the final end of the conflicting double bind between art and philosophy and between art and beauty, which had been defining their relation for a long time. This path had begun with Plato and had been revolutionized with the birth of the philosophy of art, in which the relations between art and beauty (and therefore, implicitly, between art and philosophy), had become even more strident than at the beginning.

This is a dramatic fall from the hyperuranion. Giving up any transcendent reference, rejecting ancient prerogatives claimed by philosophy over art, any unit of measurement to judge the latter is lost. But it's the very concept of artwork as *unicum* that ceases to exist. In fact, it is a tributary of a metaphysical concept—the most important of the transcendentals: the *ens*. Where does this path lead? This is the theme of the last part of the present book, dwelling on some exemplary moments of the figurative avant-garde to extrapolate the (iterative and metonymic) modalities of its constant and indefinite reproduction.

First of all, there is the energetic dissolution of the artwork, which now claims to be the sole master of itself and thus produces itself at length, from surrealism to abstract expressionism, up to pop art. The dissolution of the body of the artwork also produces its new instance: it is reborn each time from its dismembered, subconscious, formal, masteric components that have been emancipating themselves from the main body. This autonomization of its components, this way of becoming less and less an artwork, is the way in which it becomes increasingly closer to reality. And finally it is reality that wins over the artwork itself.

At this point, albeit ironically, a story started more than two thousand years ago—that of aesthetic Platonism—comes to an end. Its landing point is a metonymic icon: Andy Warhol.[29] If indeed, as the artist put it, "Coca-Cola is who we are,"[30] this is the ironic mark of the end of a two-thousand-year-old story: that of Platonism in art. Thanks to this renewed identification with the world in its here and now, the difference between being and representation has ceased to exist. But, paradoxically, it is in this way that beauty reaffirms its ancient right to rule the world. Coca-Cola is both what we drink (and, perhaps, we enjoy) and a component of our thinking as well as its order, objectively marked by the shelves of a department store. Thus Coca-Cola constitutes our collective identity.

With Warhol—albeit ironically—beauty has come to fill, once again, the position it had always had, at least as a project or a promise: that of the measure of the world in this world. Beauty stubbornly denied by the twentieth century finds its habitat at the limit—at least ideal, if not chronological—of that time. It wants to have once again the power that myth had bestowed upon it. It wants to be once again the measure of being. This is what Land Art also seems to suggest.

So, before the present devastation of the spectacle of the world, one is tempted to wonder whether this claim of beauty should actually be recognized as legitimate. Should we say yes to metaphysics to find again a measure, to feel at home in the world again? Should we take Warhol's sarcasm seriously? Perhaps. We should seek once again a measure of the world in the world, literally ecological (also thanks to neuroscience), and reformulate the ultimate destiny of the reincarnated spectre![31] Beauty is still a project. This is its legacy, which is now up to us to address.

Chapter I

The Romantic Farewell to Beauty

The Airy Premises of a Necessary Catastrophe

As we have just seen, beauty and the twentieth century are the terms of an extreme antithesis that seems to condemn the latter to an unfortunate destiny. No other century has been accused of having deliberately betrayed the canons of beauty, of having lost all faith in it embracing its opposite as an ideal, giving in to ugliness as the most wretched of sinners gives in to the devil. One is tempted to wonder not only if all of this is true, but also how it could have been possible to come to this, and who is to blame for such a big misdeed—to paraphrase the famous aphorism 125 of *The Gay Science*, where Nietzsche announces the death of God by the hand of man.[1]

Of course, one can embark on a long historical journey to wonder whether this is a specifically twentieth-century topic or rather something that was already there, latently, and that the twentieth century simply brought out. So let's take one step back, to the nineteenth: the great century of the philosophy of art: that is to say, the great century in which beauty is no longer natural, and it is not metaphysical either—it is artistic. The story, whose main events I review shortly—is very intricate and has a theoretical aspect I would like to point out immediately, as it lies at the heart of the considerations to follow. The point is this: what if beauty, precisely by becoming artistic, betrayed itself and met ugliness? That's indeed what happens in the nineteenth century under the aegis of artistic *bohème*, which bears in it the most contradictory thing there is: art proposing itself as an autonomous institution.

The starting point here is Kant's aesthetics and, in particular, the alternative between aesthetic judgment and teleological judgment—which is not taken as an alternative by Kant, but rather by his idealist and Romantic followers. The two types of judgment are not integrated as Kant wishes; upon closer inspection, they are rather sharply opposed. In the long run, this contraposition leads to the teleological judgment overcoming the aesthetic one. After all, the aesthetic judgment is afflicted by the inevitable contradiction inherent in its disinterested character, which ends up failing to account for many of its objects. In fact, as is known, the whole sphere of "adherent beauty"—encompassing almost all things that we define "beautiful," from works of art to living beings—ends up escaping disinterest and being subjected to an extrinsic finality.

In fact, we could never decide whether a living being—say, a horse—or a building are beautiful if we didn't have a precise concept in mind to define them. For these reasons, therefore, it is not surprising that the aesthetic judgment (ahistorical and aconceptual) is not what prevails in early Romanticism,[2] overshadowed by a philosophical art of which the Romantics, starting from Fichte, are the main representatives. On the other hand, the teleological judgment takes a secret path that leads further away, through Romanticism and early idealism up to its revival in contemporary art: think, for instance, of Richard Long. The teleological judgment, in fact, is sometimes the ultimate ideal of contemporary art, and we see why and how at the end of the book. What is being proposed, ahead of its time, is a new theory of the form, one that derives from the overcoming of the ancient Platonic distinction between appearance and reality on which art (and in particular, if not exclusively, art as an autonomous institution) had based its foundations. But it is better to speak more about this later, putting the matter aside for now.

As regards the birth of a philosophical art in early Romanticism, it is interesting to recall what Friedrich Schlegel wrote in his *Philosophische Lehrjahre* (*Philosophical Apprenticeship*). Among other things, he noted that Fichte is the true philosopher of art. The same can be said of Kant who, nevertheless, is perhaps (also, or even more) a philologist of nature: "The French are prominent in wit, the philosophy of nature, politics. The British in natural science, history, empiricism, sentimental poetry. Fichte is a far greater art philosopher than Kant, who is a philologist of nature."[3]

Schlegel here manifestly acknowledges his debt to Fichte, whereas Kant identifies and seems to point at a very different direction. Through Fichte, art follows the path of art rooted in the *Streben*—Schiller's moral tension. This direction, conjugating art with the instability of the yearning (Goethe stigmatized this view precisely in discussion with Schiller), is opposed by Kant: his teleological judgment seems to indicate a different way, which will be taken up only in the Romantic age.[4] In this context, Goethe and the Romantics faced each other in a confrontation of unprecedented scope and meaning.

The issue at stake is very clear on both sides: if form were to abandon life, there would be a catastrophe with unforeseeable consequences. For the side of the *Streben*, forms, animated by infinite tension, chase life, which escaped them; for Goethe and what could be defined "Romantic naturalism" from Novalis to Schelling, it is the gaze that was blurred, but things have always been the same way: the living logos has never ceased to exist. This is a conflict between real and ideal, and Goethe has been lucidly aware of it ever since his debate with Schiller, in the background of which echoes Kant's thought. In his essay "Influence of Recent Philosophy," Goethe states, in this regard:

> Due to his friendship and sympathy for me perhaps more than for his conviction, in his *Aesthetics Letters* Schiller did not treat the good Mother (Nature) with the harshness of language that had made his *Grace and Dignity* unlovable; but because I, being just as stubborn and hard-headed as him, not only exalted the superiority of Greek poetic imagination, and the poetry founded on and derived from it, but deemed this way as the only just and desirable one, he was pushed towards more thoughtful reflections, and precisely this conflict is what originated the essays on *Naive and Sentimental Poetry*. The two ways to imagine and write poetry had to adapt and recognise each other, side by side, with the same rank.
>
> So he lay the first stone of the whole new aesthetics; in fact, the adjectives *Hellenic* and *Romantic*, or any other synonym there may be, can be traced back to the point where, for the first time, there was discussion of the superiority of the real process or of the ideal procedure.[5]

As is well known, the crucial thinker for the poetics of the first Romantics is not so much Schiller—who, for Goethe, is the one who leads the way—but rather Fichte. However, Fichte's influence is introduced within a singular combination with the Platonic revival of the end of the century, of which Friedrich Schlegel himself is one of the main protagonists.[6] For Schlegel, the point is to connect ideas with life in its elusive and fundamentally ineffable nature, seeing this movement as something that is not simply negative but that should be profited from. Based on this, ideas acquire a dynamic character that leads them to achieve a connection with life itself, finding their deepest nature in

their relation to it—according to an approach that sees Plato himself as a sort
of neo-Platonic, in line with his reception at the time. In other words, ideas
must be realized in life if they don't want to misunderstand themselves and
become mere empty shells, failing their main task—that of shaping things.

In order for this not to happen, it is necessary to enact a sort of morphological revolution, joining the Platonic idea and the Kantian one, taking the idea as
the horizon of an infinite yearning for.[7] Therefore, what happens in this context?
According to what Schlegel himself states in his *Pariser Vorlesungen*, Plato is the
creator of a philosophy, not of a system. Plato's philosophy is not closed off but
answers the need of an infinite search. Philosophy can thus be represented as an
unsatisfied aspiration, an indefinite maturation of thought that does not and
cannot find a definitive structure, if not at the cost of self-betrayal:

> It has already been noted that Plato only had a philosophy, but not
> a system, and that philosophy in general is a search, an aspiration to
> science, rather than a science in itself, and this applies in particular to
> Plato's philosophy. He never gave a definitive version of his thought
> and attempted to artistically represent this eternal becoming, forma-
> tion and development of his ideas in his dialogues.[8]

This leads to the conception that not only thought but also artworks are
in constant becoming, and this happens precisely because the artwork is the
model of a form sought in life—a yearning that is itself artistic because it is
dramatic, full of tension and expectations. If the latter weren't met, the consequences would be notable. The main one would be the failure of beauty as an
ideal of a measure that is not only and not mainly artistic but—in line with
the ancient view—cosmic (all of which shows that the success of an artwork
does not concern only the artwork itself, nor does it mainly concern the art
sphere). "Art lives on its own ideal and on the possibility to embody it; but
the ideal of art is not properly artistic."[9] So, the failure of beauty should be
understood in a perspective that is essentially metaphysical, but also historical
and metaphysical at the same time, as it bears with it a present that is far from
indifferent to the end of its adventure.

Friedrich Schlegel articulates the issue with his brother in a letter dated
28 August 1793, underlining the alternative between system and ideal. He
outlines here an infinite progress, the ideal of an *unendliche Perfektibilität*, an
endless perfectibility that he would soon take up and refine in dialogue with
Condorcet:[10]

I must take into my care two things that you deny, the system and the ideal. I know that the scandalous abuse of senseless and soulless sophists has significantly dirtied these words; but you see only that and choose denial, being unjustly suspicious of the precious eloquent testimonies of our divine nobility. What we call soul in works of art (in poetry I'd rather define it as the heart), what we call spirit and ethical dignity in man, and God in creation —living connection—this is the system with regards to the concepts. There is only one real system—the great hidden eternal nature, or the truth. But if you imagine all human thought as a whole, then it becomes evident that the truth, the accomplished unity, is the inevitable direction of all thought, even though it can *never* be reached. . . . And let me add that the spirit of the system leads only to multilateralism—which may seem paradoxical, but is definitely undeniable.[11]

The idea, the form and life are thus introduced in a constant dialogue at a distance—uninterrupted and risky—between Goethe and the Romantics.[12] This dialogue does not simply involve philosophy but also art, according to a fruitful interchange between the two, of which Romanticism is in many ways the herald, and which spells out precisely in the title—echoing Goethe's *Wilhelm Meister's Apprenticeship*—of Schlegel's *Philosophical Apprenticeship (Philosophische Lehrjahre)*. Thus poetry, like philosophy, aims at the living individuality. The becoming of the form, which must open up for the living so as not to stiffen and become self-absorbed, is thus exposed to an obvious risk: that of an (almost oxymoronic) idea of an open form that must overcome its boundaries. It is a sort of revolution of the form and its intrinsic meaning. But it is not enough to focus on this level. What is at stake is not just the semantics of the form, but also its scope as a principle of the distinction of beings—both one from the other and from the chaos preceding them—according to the original Hesiodic myth of Aphrodite's birth.

Therefore, what is being announced is the need of a real morphological revolution. This is made evident by the situation of deep imbalance between being and its idea. In this way we get closer to a nihilistic abyss: the forms and the living beings are driven to a risky and fascinating game of mirrors, which transforms both, forcing them to a gruelling confrontation. The form that does not contain, that no longer grasps, looks at reality and perceives it as an endless fragmentation that it wants to resolve. Thought, looking for a renewed and newly appropriate form, is led, in turn, to an almost obligatory step: to bear upon itself the risk of fragmentation.

To learn about reality in detail in its secret, ineffable nature, thought has to become itself a fragment according to a practice that—as is well known—was widely used by Romantic authors and by Friedrich Schlegel in particular. So, the philosophy that chose fragmentation did so as it had to face the fragmentation of the world itself. Therefore, this thought speaks by a kind of extreme ontological nominalism; it looks at reality up into its infinitesimal traits; and, to promote its own path, it adopts not a conceptual principle but a new morphological ideal, assuming in this context the appearance of one last bastion against the advance of nihilism—that is, of the dynamics and centrifugal instances of modernity, so compelling as to escape any formal control.

Facing fragmentation, paradoxically this thought must not only make an extreme unifying gesture, that of a sudden unification of the *disiecta membra* through projects such as a new Bible, the total work of art, the book of books, etc.[13] In fact, in this way it also it carries out an absolutely unusual metaphorical power, bringing together everything with everything, echoing the different elements through contacts and unusual harmonies. On the other hand, the metaphor can be overturned into catachresis, thus recognizing the failure of form in its going back to itself, no longer able to accommodate its content, and thereby destined to wrap itself up in a tautological self-reflection.

This is certainly one of the risks of the Romantic art form that is highlighted by Hegel (who predates the phenomenon by locating the birth of modernity in Christianity),[14] but this also coincides with a dilation of the borders and meaning of the problem of the form according to an orientation that—as we see better in the next chapter—is adopted by Nietzsche. In fact, Nietzsche saw nihilism as essentially a sort of *formal failure*, the logoi falling back on themselves. Indeed, for Nietzsche, nihilism is nothing more than this: the irredeemable autonomization of the logoi from reality, so that they fall back on themselves as pale, inert, and powerless forms, while being develops a wild and conflictual nature under the guise of the will to power.

This almost definitely marks the final disappearance of Goethe's viewpoint and his passionate defense of the continuity of art, idea, and nature. Thus disappears the possibility to refer to models or types as Goethe had done by resorting to the idea of the original plant and that of the intermaxillary bone: those were ideas that unified the spheres of plant and animal nature, thereby also allowing them to differentiate themselves. What happens here is a sort of major catastrophe: it is the end of that poetic and poietic side of thought, connected with the idea and therefore with the form, on which the Romantic gaze had focused. Thus, what is lost is the intuition that marks thought from its very beginning and without which thought could not even work, or at least communicate.

Form, Style, Entropy

Returning now to the antithesis set out above between aesthetic judgment and teleological judgment and taking it to its extreme consequences, one would argue that if the aesthetic judgment gives rise to autonomous art, understood as an institution in its own right, the teleological judgment originates the inextricable interweaving between art and nature that seems to be the hidden reason, the fertile remorse, of aesthetics and reflection on art in the twentieth century. Friedrich Schlegel, Novalis, and Schelling seem to initiate the great battle between aesthetic judgment and teleological judgment. As we have seen, victory immediately (at least provisionally) goes to the former.

It's as if there was a slow and—at least in Schlegel—still uncertain growth of a seed sown in the first introduction to the *Critique of Judgment*, which brings us to Romanticism through the idea of a "technique of nature." This can be inferred from Schlegel's already-cited philosophical notebooks, for instance when he states—against the Kantian view on the purely regulative nature of the idea of finality—that the technique of nature is an integral part of the theory of ends, thereby asseverating the continuity of nature and culture. The theory of ends constitutes, in turn, a part of historiography, of the discipline whose object is the human story and its aims. "*Historiography* is divided in the *doctrine of ends* and the *doctrine of culture*. We should not transpose the technicality of nature into mankind—or rather, it also belongs to the *doctrine of ends*."[15]

But what Schlegel emphasises is the constructive character of Kant's doctrine, showing— for instance—that experience is not a given but something constructed. On this basis one must also understand Schlegel's doctrine of art:

> Kant does not start from the fact that *experience* IS, according to a misunderstanding that was also shared by *Niethammer, Reinhold, Erhard*; but from the unproven—and yet to be demonstrated—proposition that *experience* MUST BE, according to what Beck, Fichte and Schelling have rightly understood. This proposition must absolutely be demonstrated.[16]

The constructed character of experience refers us back to the artificial character of art itself, in contraposition to the Kantian technique of nature. This is a crucial point, one that affects the entire path I wish to address in this book. Just as experience, art also can be said to be related to something constructed. And constructed art—the construction of art—inevitably clashes against beauty. In short, one could also say that the twentieth-century negation of the beautiful—which is, if not the object, at least the origin of all those considerations—is rooted much earlier, in that crucial passage in which aesthetics became philosophy of art. The birth of the philosophy of art, the pair art-historical knowledge—which already somewhat appeared in the abovementioned dialogue between Schiller and Goethe—actually means the disappearance of beauty that, as such (as a witness and a compendium of the intrinsic measure of the cosmos) is not and cannot be artificial or constructed.

When, in the *Aesthetics: Lectures on, Fine Art*, Hegel speaks of the end of art, at least "considered in its highest vocation," he is essentially acknowledging what I have just explained. If beauty (even artistic) is no longer the compendium of the cosmic law but expresses its own, it condemns itself to fading, to becoming a side phenomenon in the cosmos of culture, bowing to the unstoppable power of the concept. For Hegel all of this is intrinsic to the becoming of the spirit:

> Only one sphere and stage of truth is capable of being represented in the element of art. In order to be a genuine content for art, such truth must in virtue of its own specific character be able to go forth into [the sphere of] sense and remain adequate to itself there. This is the case, for example, with the gods of Greece. [. . .] Thought and reflection have spread their wings above fine art. [. . .] It is not, as might be supposed, merely that the practising artist himself is infected by the loud voice of reflection all around him and by the opinions and judgements on art that have become customary everywhere, so that he is misled into introducing more thoughts into his work; the point is that our whole spiritual culture is of such a kind that he himself stands within the world of reflection and its relations, and could not by any act of will and decision abstract himself from it; nor could he by special education or removal from the relations of life contrive and organize a special solitude to replace what he has lost.
>
> In all these respects art, considered in its highest vocation, is and remains for us a thing of the past. Thereby it has lost for us

genuine truth and life, and has rather been transferred into our ideas instead of maintaining its earlier necessity in reality and occupying its higher place.[17]

At a closer look, beauty goes down with the rise of the philosophy of art, when the attention gets organized around the aesthetic object, which replaces the eighteenth-century aesthetics founded on sentiment.[18] Artistic beauty is always the product of becoming, something made and never simply given to the person who contemplates it. To reformulate this thesis once again, one could say that the autonomy of the beautiful—which Goethe saw as a threat—coincides with its very disappearance. And this is the tragic background against which the philosophy of art was born. This is also the starting point of all the considerations included here.

Besides, the naturalness of beauty is related—and here we come to the classicistic paradigm and its highest model—to a natural balance of forces in which the effort of the construction is not (or should not be) felt. This is precisely what Winckelmann writes about in his very famous description of *Laocoon* in his *Reflections on the Painting and Sculpture of the Greeks*. This is precisely what Schlegel becomes aware of in his great youthful essay "On the Study of Greek Poetry," where he senses the loss of the ancient balance.

Let's start from Winckelmann's description of *Laocoon* to test our thesis. His text couldn't be any more exemplary and eloquent (nor could it be any more famous).

The last and most eminent characteristic of the Greek works is a noble simplicity and sedate grandeur in Gesture and Expression. As the bottom of the sea lies peaceful beneath a foaming surface, a great soul lies sedate beneath the strife of passions in Greek figures.

'Tis in the face of Laocoon this soul shines with full lustre, amidst the most violent sufferings. Pangs piercing every muscle, every labouring nerve; pangs which we almost feel ourselves, while we consider—not the face, nor the most expressive parts—only the belly contracted by excruciating pains: these however, I say, exert not themselves with violence, either in the face or gesture. He pierces not heaven, like the Laocoon of *Virgil*.[19]

Following Peter Szondi,[20] one can overturn this image and, reversing the depth-surface order proposed by Winckelmann, one can see passions as a potentially turbulent element that manages to redeem itself from its deep disquiet by turning to the surface in search of the levity of the form. Well, in this way the classical model represented by *Laocoon* also eliminates energy losses; it generates the highly improbable balance that we call "order," a useful compendium of forces in the form. It is as if there were a system of forces and counterforces that manage to balance each other at a key point that balances and compensates the opposing tensions. That's how this tempering of forces in the form described by Winckelmann might well be summed up by the words of Rudolph Arnheim reported below, unrelated to any specific examples:

> Now equilibrium is the very opposite of disorder. A system is in equilibrium when the forces constituting it are arranged in such a way as to compensate each other, like the two weights pulling at the arms of a pair of scales. Equilibrium makes for standstill—no further action can occur, except by outside influence.[21]

It is not hard to glimpse in those presuppositions a sort of entropic direction of art going hand in hand with its formal dissolution. The elements of the form now tend to break free from the constraints imprisoning them, mingling with each other and making it collapse. The energies that structure the work of art also tend to escape from it, and they do so in order to identify themselves ecstatically with that life, which they should subsequently reshape through a perfect transposition. One consequence is the emergence of the ugly as a characteristic element of modern art, which derives precisely from this escape, from the dispersion of the elements conglomerated in the formal structure and catalyzed by the latter, which provided them with a keystone.

In the transition to this new formal structure, in this time of crisis and disorder, the ugly appears. The advent of ugliness is the outcome of the transformation of aesthetics into energy: the dispersion of the elements structuring the form frees the energies that organized them. Ugliness is therefore also brutal, deriving from the imbalance of the forces giving rise to formal structure, which thus violently break away from it. This justifies the morbid interest of aesthetic modernity in figures such as Frankenstein and Moosbrugger! The ugly comes from the dissolved balance of the energies in form. In contrast—as is exemplarily illustrated by Winckelmann's passage mentioned above—form is a time of stabilization of energy conflicts, which proposes itself as definitive, at least as it cannot be altered by endogenous causes but only through outside interventions.

Herein, in the perfect unchangeable internal balance, lies the perfection of classic art, which also makes it intangible. The loss of form does not represent only a failure; it also coincides with an increase in available energy, thus crediting a dynamic propensity that is peculiar to the first German Romanticism and based on which the concept of chaos acquires a significant meaning in modern art.[22]

Thus the way was paved to a new, conflictual, model of beauty and to the avant-garde: that is, the consciously antagonistic formal dynamic used, for example, by futurism but also by artists such as Kandinsky. It must be said that the first signs of this journey—as the reader probably remembers—appeared long before, already in the first major work by Friedrich Schlegel, which manifests (under the sign of the triumph of the ugly) an aesthetic model marked by conflicts and lacerations that questions Winckelmann's, nearly constituting its oppositional *pendant*. The formal structure has opened up—for Schlegel—freeing the forces that compose it in a disorderly and craving manner. These forces thus arrange themselves in a confrontational way that is reflected in the ugly. This, as the reader surely recalls, is the wasteland of aesthetic modernity, crossed by turbulent energies whose struggle never reaches the tranquillity of a solid formal structure.

What truly happened? Knowing this is useful to understand how much of the Romantic legacy has survived till the twentieth century, contributing to its aesthetic consciousness. Through Schlegel's dramatic passages the principle of the artwork has fallen.[23] The principle of the author and authorship—linked to it by conceptual symmetry—has fallen with it. However, the relation between the two cannot immediately appear evident; on the contrary, Romanticism was often accused by its great opponents (especially Goethe and Hegel) of excessively emphasizing subjectivity. The crisis of the subject and the crisis of the object—as imprecise as the terminology may be—also go hand in hand, as shown not only by Romanticism but also by modernity.

The crisis of the former goes together with that of the latter. We are dealing with a pair of terms or a hendiadys that—like Goethe's *Urpflanze*—creates further, almost infinite ones: breakout of subjectivity and language, possibility to communicate, and universality of the subject, style and sublime,[24] decorum and expression, all full of meaning for the future. We are witnessing the emergence of a double movement that, on the one hand, refers to formal rigor and, on the other, relates to the ideal of an artwork that lies beyond its objective reality. Thus is produced what could be defined as a fall out of the form, with the neurotic and almost reactive counterweight of the communicative and ideologically unambiguous objectivity of the style (up until stylistic terrorism, the obtuse and almost caricature-like neo-classicism of dictatorships, especially national socialism). In the latter case the stylistic order prefigures and affirms the real one.[25]

As Hans Belting noted, this does not happen insofar as the ideal of the artwork goes beyond the artwork itself, realizing—I would add—what Romantic Platonism has always suggested. It is also true that the artwork opens up in two directions: both towards its ideal and towards an ambiguous infinity, which is not only the beyond to which the work tends but also its very origin. These are not only artworks alluding to something beyond figuration according to the varied tradition of the sublime, from Caspar David Friedrich to Marcel Duchamp, Ives Klein, or Barnett Newman. Indeed, we can probably also reconstruct a tradition going back to a sort of prebreak, which happens not after its configuration but at the origin of form: think of authors such as Philipp Otto Runge[26] or—to come to the twentieth century—of movements such as action painting, which I address in the last chapter.

I come back to these considerations, but for now I wish to return to German Romanticism to grasp the main traits of the whole journey. It is easy to see that the limits and structure of the artwork suffer a deep crisis. But to understand this crisis even better, one should resort to one of the central tenets of modern hermeneutics. I am referring to a classic theme of the theory of the interpretation of a literary text; not surprisingly, that's what leads us up until the limits of chaos understood as the beginning of understanding. I am referring to the idea—articulated in different ways by Friedrich Schlegel and then by Schleiermacher—that an author should be understood by her audience better than she understands herself.

When Friedrich Schlegel and then Schleiermacher formulated a proposal of this kind, they foresaw the need for a genetic process by which the personality (at the least the conscious one) of the author must recede in front of a deeper and earlier demand. For Schleiermacher this demand is met in a psychological identification in the authorial *iter*;[27] and for Schlegel it is a sort of chaotic area preceding any psychological requirement. Chaos becomes the principle of being and creation, as can be inferred from this passage from "On Incomprehensibility": "Verily, it would fare badly with you if, as you demand, the world were ever to become wholly comprehensible in earnest. And isn't this entire, unending world constructed by the understanding out of incomprehensibility or chaos?"[28]

Decorum and Expression

The antithesis taking shape here leads towards the dissolution of the form and subjectivity as correlated principles of the articulation of the artwork. To delve into the issue, it is perhaps appropriate to implement a pictorial distinction dating back to the sixteenth-century treatises: that between design and color. Such distinction echoed significantly in the Romantic context, thanks to an essay by August Wilhelm Schlegel, "Die Gemälde," originally published in *Athenäum* in 1799: in it, painting emancipates itself from other plastic arts (architecture and sculpture) as an eminently modern art. This is a significant detachment, because it sets the objective, plastic, sculptural aspect of painting against the subjective, expressive, properly pictorial one, which is rooted in perspective and color.[29] To translate this contraposition in terms useful for the purposes of this book, one must say that in many ways the journey of aesthetic modernity leads to the divorce between the two aspects that give the title to this paragraph: expression, connected to subjectivity, and decorum in its stylistic and monumental appearance. The contraposition of the two terms also leads to a decay of both: taken to its limits, the expressiveness of the subject is lost in the ineffability stigmatized by Hegel, while an absolute monumentality loses sight of the life that should nurture it as an artistic event.

Now, the balance of these two aspects and its subsequent crisis actually hints at a broader balance, which also seems to have been undermined. The encounter between the stylistic-monumental aspect with the subjective-expressive one is the compendium of opposing forces, ones that in the Romantic culture go by different names: ancient and modern, Greek and Christian. For many of the protagonists of the so-called age of Goethe,[30] the Renaissance unified those themes; but the subsequent history separated them again, thus rendering the ancient model an exclusively stylistic one, classicism, while the modern became a subjective hyperbole that can alternately, but also indifferently, produce both hypertrophy—the limitless power of the subject—and ineffable mysticism.

In many ways—if I may provisionally use an expression so broad and generic—the fate of modern art is sealed by this oscillation between opposites, between the emergence of the individual and monumentality, and by the nihilistic crisis that comes from their impossible union. The subject and the world become each other's alternative without being able to interrupt their relationship.[31] Indeed, this relation continues with an insistence that is neurotic but also, in hindsight, fertile. In this way the two terms of this difficult relationship—which are no longer able to establish some stable contact but which repeatedly seek it—produce the dissipative trend described above. Because the form does not take on a conclusive and accomplished appearance, it still leaves free part of the energies that tend to organize it; and these become, paradoxically but also fruitfully, cause for further dispersion. The latter increases the metamorphic transformation process in the frustrating but paradoxically also productive search of another form, again inevitably inadequate in relation to what it has to display and contain.

So—to take a step from Romanticism to the avant-garde—this is the configuration of forms with conflicting traits. Precisely because they are open forms, anticlassical ones, they turn, despite themselves, into their opposite: they cease being proud representatives of the autonomy of art and become deliberately voted to its decline, to an infinite emptiness, which should finally rejoin the life from which they have claimed to have freed themselves.[32] The dialectic between form and life, brilliantly initiated by Schlegel in his early Platonic studies—in other words, the effort that leads to their impossible union and that must be properly understood as energetic (both dissipating and creating energy)—produces a persistent oscillation from pole to pole.

The form is forced to deal with the details of existence, experiencing life as objective dispersion, which revolutionizes it, disrupting its composition and its balances. It is forced to take a plastic attitude opposed to reality in its unrestrainable aspect, albeit risking breaking against the latter. The form should attract life, saving it from the disenchantment of time and of the end, providing it with the chrism of eternity, but instead ends up collapsing on life itself, no longer able to be distinguished from it. This is the tragedy of the formal dynamic, which would like to attract the living and instead is sucked into it following a parabola that has its climax far beyond German Romanticism—that is, as mentioned, in Andy Warhol. Indeed when Warhol ironically suggests that our collective identity is Coca-Cola, he is sanctioning the end of a story that—to mention only its modern side—has lasted for nearly two centuries.

Warhol is discussed in the last chapter. For now let's follow the form in its neurotic developments. Art longs to return to life and seeks again a classicity that (at least for now) is impossible.

Chapter II

The Non-containing Form

From Nietzsche to Spengler

Mimesis and Descriptive Knowledge

In the conclusions to the previous chapter, I hinted at the possibility that the twentieth century, so to speak, might have dusted off and updated the topic of morphological reason as it was developed, at least at first, in the German culture of the late eighteenth century, thanks largely to Goethe. What do I mean here by "morphological reason"? I am referring to the model of reason for which the idea, the principle of form, lurks in reality and therefore can be found in it—with a reversed intuitive approach, in terms of rational articulation, not on the conceptual level but on the descriptive one.[1] This is certainly the model à la Goethe that echoes up until the early twentieth century. It must be emphasized that this is, so to speak—as we see later—a cross pattern that ends up unifying fundamentally different dimensions: from science to Thomas Mann's ideal writing, which clearly shows the confidence that the adhesion to the object will reveal its intimate structure and underlying order.[2]

The ideal of description can help only on the presupposition that the particular points to the universal or the type without which we would be lost without hope of ever finding our way in the infinite variety of the world. This is indeed the ideal underpinning the novel and its mimetic relationship with reality, so that what is humble is exalted, the last things become the first, and the trivialities of the most anodyne life rise to the dignity of narrative. All of this was very lucidly emphasised by György Lukács (who, nevertheless, shows great consistency in his path from *The Theory of the Novel* to the unfortunate outcomes of his last aesthetics).[3] Here one can notice a sort of classical mimetic coherence: an Aristotelian connection between mimesis and knowledge, so that the former trusts to find the type in the particular.[4]

This is a principle of order that spreads in the theory of literary genres and becomes a system, thanks to the latter. It is a link that, after having been undermined by Romanticism, will definitively break with the avant-garde which—as is all too well known—abandons the ideal of mimesis, the privileged relationship with the first nature, replacing it with the ideal of creating a second, "other" nature. It is the sign of an unbridgeable gap. Let's try to anticipate it briefly before analyzing it in a more comprehensive way. This journey is anything but devoid of ambivalent turns. In fact, the ideal of mimesis, in hindsight, was anything but defeated at the end of this affair; it rather got lost in an ambivalent aesthetic dimension: illustrative, decorative, ornamental; and this depends on the fact that the relationship between mimesis and knowledge was definitely interrupted.

This is the rise of mass art, not only in the literal sense, but also in that of a universal decorative instinct that flows into advertising, which offers every object as unique, making it iridescent and, so to speak, irrevocable. But there's more. One could risk an educated hypothesis related to the art-knowledge link proposed by the issue of mimesis. That is, one could say that the mimetic ideal ends up being at one with historical knowledge, which aims to reinvest the ideal of description with the universal scope long entrusted to the novel (we see this shortly with Dilthey).

On the other hand, this ideal seems to fail precisely in one of the areas of natural science favored by Goethe, that of biology: according to the great Darwinian biologist Ernst Haeckel, it showed an increasing propensity to nominalism, which makes it impossible to classify species. The central point here is surely the fact that the failure of scientific classification paves the way to a sort of aestheticization of science, with consequences in the long run. As happens with goods, offering a sort of paradoxical serial uniqueness, even animal organisms become decorative elements that attract the curiosity of the general public through popular publications,[5] but also through motifs such as Van de Velde's jellyfish, derived from Haeckel's biological studies.[6] This is the beginning of a long journey in the aestheticism of scientific knowledge, which results in very recent times in such films as *Jurassic Park*.[7]

Let's try to find passages in between the structures of knowledge using aesthetics as a privileged observatory, which allows us to transit in different areas along the seams suggested by the principle of form.

From Goethe to Dilthey

Our starting point must be the path from Goethe to Nietzsche up to Spengler, which we must try to outline or catch a glimpse of the outcomes. Sticking to a Goethean framework—which can take us rather far—we might say that what's at stake here is the descriptive character of reason. In fact, if one traces the path that goes from Goethe to Nietzsche, one can see a route that bears within itself, at least from two points of view, the decline of what could be called "morphological reason." At one level this is due to the difficulty—suffered by Nietzsche—to approximate the form, in its stability, to being as fragmented and subject to dispersion over time.

One might say that the synthesis of particulars in a whole that was announced by Goethe fails with Nietzsche. For the latter, forms and time are destined not to meet each other ever again—contrary to what seemed to be possible with Goethe or with Schelling's philosophy of identity. No new Renaissance can be thought of or even wished for. The Romantic "morphological crisis" is now complete: forms can no longer find their way to the heart of being to give it some stability. This broken continuity affects in many ways the possibility of uniting old and new from both a historical-epochal and a purely typological-formal point of view. Nor can the two aspects be split off from each other. It is the historic failure that causes, entails, and produces the crisis of the idea or type that—as is seen below—goes by the name of "nihilism."

To briefly anticipate what follows, "nihilism" can be defined as a decline of the form, which is no longer recognized as their own by the individuals it should contemplate within itself: they thus find themselves in a crisis concerning their very self-recognition, their common identity founded on similarity to and difference from others. In this way, devoid of terms of comparison and significant references to introduce it in that completed mutual references system that is the cosmos, individuality becomes increasingly individualized, gradually approaching particularity, discovering ineffability in its intrinsic transience.

As we have seen in the previous chapter, this is where the Romantic crisis takes place, or better, this is the wellspring of Romanticism as the conscious epicenter of this earthquake. With this perspective, we have access to the unfolding of a story that runs through the history of concepts as a sort of autonomous power, almost regardless of the thinkers who are its protagonists. As for the characters of this story, we go way beyond Nietzsche, up until the extreme twentieth-century revival of Goethe represented by Oswald Spengler. The form is tackled here under different profiles: from the metaphysical to the aesthetic one (on which I dwell the longest). However, there is also the political aspect, where the form, by virtue of its capacity, is also the example of a real community while outlining the possible one.

Nietzsche and the Decline of Form

Let us go through the issue in its fundamental articulations starting from Nietzsche and, in particular, from the *Antichrist*. Before dwelling on this, though, I would briefly go back to the origins of the problem in Nietzsche.[8] In this context one cannot forget that Nietzsche did not assume from the outset that the Greek legacy and the modern, the ancient and the Christian, forms and time are set one against the other—as one can instead draw from his later thought, condemning Christianity as a fatal laceration, as a kind of drain of mythopoietic resources, which were powerful and flourishing in ancient Greece. Embracing such a conclusion means thinking that Western culture has faced an unprecedented catastrophe, which has a philosophical name: nihilism.

From this standpoint, nihilism is but the acknowledgment that the dual root of European culture (the Greek and the Jewish) is the cause of an unbridgeable gap that will lead to the dissolution of that very culture. That is to say: one cannot put together faith in stability and the form (attributed to classical Greece) and the time acceleration characterizing modernity, oriented towards its eschatological finality. No good can come from this contradiction: the attempt at conciliation made by the Weimarian classics and by their Romantic antagonists has led to the end of the age of both. This outcome is due to the fact that both parties cultivated this excessive hope, which has also produced an optimistic and eudaimonistic distortion of Greek thought, as Nietzsche lucidly noted.[9]

It is worth remembering in this context that Nietzsche did not always have this opinion: at his gymnasium, in Schulpforta, he was criticized because of his suspicious passion for a poet such as Hölderlin, who had been ensnared in the darkness of madness.[10] And Hölderlin's thesis is completely the opposite of what the last Nietzsche posits. Compare *Bread and Wine* with the ending of *Ecce Homo*: these theoretical assumptions do not just clash, but are totally opposite. In fact, in *Bread and Wine* we find the last link between Christ and Dionysus in the Eucharistic symbology of the bread and the wine. In *Ecce Homo*, as is well known, this is completely overturned into the sharpest antithesis, in a display of anti-Christianity that is as violent as it is ambiguous and ambivalent: "Was I understood?—*Dionysus versus the Crucified*."[11] This statement acts as a paradoxical antithetic *pendant* to what Nietzsche himself wrote in his youthful diaries, focusing on his roots: "As a plant I was born close to the churchyard, and as a human being in a vicarage."[12]

Something very important has changed in Nietzsche's journey, and it is something related to the original project of the *Moderne*, to the glimpse of the synthesis between ancient and modern outlined in the idealistic age—probably starting from Schelling's comment to Plato's *Timaeus*.[13] The impossible bond that should join time and evidence, reinstating the unity of forms in time—the paradoxical stylistic unity of the *Moderne*—seems to definitely break down in Nietzsche's thought. The here and now that refracts the eternal in time and that can still be sensed in the pages of Schelling's *Philosophy of Art*, as a symbol of a new Renaissance inaugurated by the Romantics, undergoes the most extreme and conscious defeat in Nietzsche—a defeat so clear that it is difficult to say whether it is possible to get up again after such a disastrous fall.

The pressure of time of an eschatologically marked universe cannot contain the intelligence inherent in the evidence of the ancient form. And intelligence here means style, unity of artistic style connoting an era as a whole, allowing it to be contemplated with a single glance.[14] Through its morphological connotations, art thus acquires a decisive significance within this landscape, which allows it to go well beyond the insulation of aesthetic consciousness. It is a position that art acquires both positively and negatively: both in defining the present situation in its broken fragmentariness, and in indicating the medicine able to cure everything.

This obviously goes beyond any atheistic thread that could be found in Nietzsche's thought. Far from being a profession of atheism, in fact, Nietzsche's reflection rather uses religion as a parameter to judge a civilization. This clarifies the terms of the issue. Nietzsche's relationship with Christianity should not be understood only or exclusively in the sense of his belonging or nonbelonging to that religion (of which, in any case, he sees himself as an integral part), but also, and perhaps above all, in the context of a story that is just as intense as, and inextricably linked to, the previous one.

I am referring to the link between the religion itself (any religion, not just the Christian one) to an artistic and mythopoietic issue, so to speak. This is the real parameter by which Nietzsche looks at religion and its significance. The articulation of judgment becomes extremely complex in this area, as it is based on their mythopoietic qualities that religions are evaluated. And this mythopoietic quality has a name: "will to power." With his *outré* spirit voted to linguistic paradox (which makes him so close to the early twentieth century), Nietzsche celebrates the hot blooded and creative arrogance of Cesare Borgia, while condemning the bloodless nature of Protestantism, from which he himself comes. Nietzsche says in the sixteenth paragraph of the *Antichrist*:

> A nation that still believes in itself holds fast to its own god. In him it does honour to the conditions which enable it to survive, to its virtues—it projects its joy in itself, its feeling of power, into a being to whom one may offer thanks. He who is rich will give of his riches; a proud people need a god to whom they can make sacrifices. . . . Religion, within these limits, is a form of gratitude. A man is grateful for his own existence: to that end he needs a god.—Such a god must be able to work both benefits and injuries; he must be able to play either friend or foe—he is wondered at for the good he does as well as for the evil he does. But the castration, against all nature, of such a god, making him a god of goodness alone, would be contrary to human inclination. [. . .]—True enough, when a nation is on the downward path, when it feels its belief in its own future, its hope of freedom slipping from it, when it begins to see submission as a first necessity and the virtues of submission as measures of self-preservation, then it—must—overhaul its god. [. . .] He moralizes endlessly; he creeps into every private virtue; he becomes the god of every man; he becomes a private citizen, a cosmopolitan. [. . .] Formerly he represented a people, the strength of a people, everything aggressive and thirsty for power in the soul of a people; now he is simply the good god. . . . The truth is that there is no other alternative for gods: either they are the will to power—in which case they are national gods—or incapacity for power—in which case they have to be good.[15]

As Jacob Taubes notes, Nietzsche attacks Paul's *sermo humilis*, using as a *locus classicus* Corinthians 1:20ff. and considering the folly of the cross as exemplary of a morality that arises from resentment and the spirit of revenge.[16] Beauty becomes in this context a polemical aim of Christianity, which is consistently followed—as is well known—by all the other Nietzschean criticisms: the devaluation of nature, instincts, etc. As is not difficult to understand, it is a deeply consistent negative sequence, which implies that Christianity, for Nietzsche, programmatically occludes the roots of sensibility and therefore of intuition.

Christianity privileges innerness, giving a purely allegoric value to nature and reality. In short, Christianity is guilty on two parallel levels that can be summed up as the idea that giving up the resources of sensibility makes it so that time and space, as well as time and eternity (which embodies time's supreme yearning for extension), are opposed to each other once and for all, with no possible compensation. This, for Nietzsche, is an unprecedented catastrophe: time no longer finds in itself the elements that induce it to moments of tranquillity and stasis. In other words, the coagulation of being we call "reality" no longer exists. It is the peak of the nihilistic crisis.

To put this differently, using terms pertaining to aesthetics that are also useful to outline the age in question, now it is no longer possible to go from force to form, so that the forces are conflictingly dispersed opposing each other. This phenomenon takes the shape of the will to power that, only in this context, is revealed as such: an energy quantum exclusively aimed to its self-affirmation. In this case, forces are no longer able to follow a virtuous path that allows going from chaos to form. They can no longer arrange that system of drives and counterdrives which sees the threat of conflict as the source of a harmonic configuration, as instead happened in Winckelmann's description of the *Laocoon*: the latter is perhaps the best example of the classical vocation to order understood as optimization of the energies in play. In fact, as we have seen, the form contemplated by the formula of "noble simplicity" and "sedate grandeur" is such insofar as it avoids chaos and energy conflict. When, on the other hand, its components are dispersed, they enhance their presumed individuality in their extreme autonomy, in separation from any type: this makes them equal only to themselves and finally, necessarily, each ends up being aggressive against all others. With the decline of the form, therefore, what occurs is something similar to what happens with the disintegration of empires: the parties turn against the whole and—once the whole has fallen—against each other!

As you can see—leaving politics aside—the contiguity between different spheres is particularly evident in this context: the passage from aesthetics to religion to metaphysics and the other way round is here almost immediate. To put it very simply, time—the eschatological temporality introduced by the Jewish-Christian world—comes into conflict with the legacy of the Greek measure, which is placed in the idea of the cosmos and provides that intuitive balance that lies in the concept of beauty. Nietzsche's is an exemplary journey, one that illustrates a kind of living continuity within his thought. It starts from the *Birth of Tragedy*, where Nietzsche tries to show—resorting to ancient tragedy and with Wagner's help—that the passage from the force to the form cannot happen only in ancient Greece but also in the Christian *Moderne,* where the subject (and not the object) prevails. Going from the energetic and chaotic dimension of the Dionysian to the accomplished form of the Apollonian is not only possible: it properly generates a civilization—the tragic civilization that Nietzsche sees as the model of any culture to come.

Thus another constant element of Nietzsche's thought emerges: the idea that religiosity and culture are very closely related—which allows one to reconsider the whole of his theoretical path. However, to go back to our starting point, it is surely evident that the final crisis of Nietzsche's thought is ultimately related precisely to the search (impossible today) for the connection between time and evidence. The fragments of the last period reproduce precisely—in an almost hallucinatory fashion—the idea of an impossible union of time and evidence; it looms in the guise of the eternal return, which is the last, almost caricature-like, attempt to give some regularity to the impetuous advance of time:

> If the world could in any way become rigid, dry, dead, *nothing,* or if it could reach a state of equilibrium, or if it had any kind of goal that involved duration, immutability, the once-and-for-all (in short, speaking metaphysically: if becoming could resolve itself into being or into nothingness), *then this state must have been reached:* from which it follows. [. . .] If the world may be thought of as a certain definite quantity of force and as a certain definite number of centers of force—and every other representation remains indefinite and therefore useless—it follows that, in the great dice game of existence, it must pass through calculable number of combinations. In infinite time, every possible combination would at some time or another be realized; more: it would be realized an infinite number of times. And since between every combination and its next recurrence all other possible combinations would have to take place, and each of these combination conditions of the entire sequence of combinations in the same series, a circular movement of absolutely identical series is thus demonstrated: the world as a circular movement that has already repeated itself infinitely often and plays its game *in infinitum.* [17]

The desperate attempt to introduce once again elements of tranquillity and relative stability—this time not under the Greek sky but under the modern one, marked by the thunders of time acceleration—produces a monstrous creation, which cannot go back to the crystal clearness of the form. What Winckelmann described in the *Laocoon*—the virtuous system of drives and counter-drives that has its keystone in the form, where the conflict is stabilized with no winners or losers—can no longer happen. Thus Nietzsche states:

> And do you know what the "world" is to me? Shall I show you in my mirror? This world: a monster of energy, without beginning, without end; a firm, iron magnitude of force that does not grow bigger or smaller, that does not expend itself but only transforms itself; as a whole, of unalterable size, a household without expenses or losses, but likewise without increase or income; enclosed by "nothingness" as by a boundary; not something blurry or wasted, not something endlessly extended, but set in a definite space as a definite force, and not a space that might be "empty" here or there, but rather as force throughout, as a play of forces and waves of forces, at the same time one and many, increasing here and at the same time decreasing there; a sea of forces flowing and rushing together, eternally changing, eternally flooding back, with tremendous years of recurrence, with an ebb and a flood of its forms; out of the simplest forms striving toward the most complex, out of the stillest, most rigid, coldest forms striving toward the hottest, most turbulent, most self-contradictory, and then again returning home to the simple out of this abundance, out of the play of contradictions back to the joy of concord, still affirming itself in this uniformity of its courses and its years, blessing itself as that which must return eternally, as a becoming that knows no satiety, no disgust, no weariness.[18]

It is clear now that temporality has lost all relation to evidence. The Jewish eschatological legacy has engulfed the Greek heritage, depriving the universal forms of all evidence and intelligibility. There are only individuals assigned to their nakedness, which is essentially a sign of their unrelatedness; they are strangers to each other because there is no type that unites them. It is, as it were, a real monadological revolution that will culminate in the absolute idiosyncratic expression, thus paving the way—or at least one of the ways—to artistic avant-garde.[19]

From Nietzsche to Goethe and Beyond

This is a long journey, which will take us through Goethe and Nietzsche to Haeckel and Dilthey, up until twentieth-century artistic avant-garde. But let's go back to Goethe for a moment. In his brief text on morphology, he claimed,

"Morphology must contain the theory of the form, formation and transformation of organic bodies; therefore, it belongs to the natural sciences of which we are illustrating the purposes. Natural history assumes as a matter of fact the multiplicity of forms of organisms."[20]

Therefore, the point is to grasp living forms in their connection, which is in turn lived and arranged in the order of the visible, where the form institutes the relation between the two poles (the living and the visible), and the same goes for the morphological continuity between nature and art.[21]

Besides, Goethe's form is not *one*: it is rather a multiplicity striving for unity, while the latter tends to divide itself so as to take different configurations. The Goethean form is threatened by the accumulation of particulars so that, when there is an overcrowding of the latter (which in principle are infinite) it collapses, producing at the same time the haemorrhagic escape of its components, which gives rise to the ugly. To reconstruct the issue, it is worth looking at the following passage of the short essay "On Spinoza":

> All limited lives are in the infinite, and yet not by being part of the infinite, but rather participating of infinity. [. . .] What we call parts of a living being are so inseparable from the whole that the parts themselves can only be understood in and with the whole; and neither the parts can be used as a measure of the whole, nor the whole as a measure of the parts. Therefore, as has been said previously, we argue that a limited living being participates of the infinite, or better, it has something infinite in itself, if one does not want to argue that we cannot fully understand the concept of existence and perfection of a living being, even the most limited one, and therefore we have to consider it as infinite as the immense whole in which all existences are included.[22]

In another short and well-known essay, "Die Absicht Eingeleitet," Goethe notes that the form, the *Gestalt*, is not as immobile as the term might lead one to believe. In fact, as I mentioned above, it is not *one* either: it is rather derived from a myriad of components that, by principle, are infinite:

> Every living thing is not a single entity, but a plurality; despite appearing as an individual, it remains a set of living and autonomous beings that, equal according to the idea and by nature, appear empirically identical or similar, different or dissimilar. These beings are partly

united at their origin, and have partly found each other and joined later; they split and seek each other again, generating an endless production in every way and in every direction.[23]

So the differentiation of the parts itself is the principle of their assimilation in the set of living things, while their subordination rather relates to the completeness of a creature. But what is the same according to the idea—adds Goethe—may appear as similar or dissimilar or even unequal; and this is precisely typical of the "animated pace of nature." The dissimilar assimilates according to the idea; and this is therefore the principle of the living form, whose ineffable individuality is defined on the basis of its intimate complexity—namely, on the basis of the fabric of relations, in principle infinite, that constitute it.[24]

This is the field of physiology, but it also refers to an axiological dimension realized by formal completeness; in the same context, furthermore, the pathological takes a negative moral value—according to Goethe in *Nacharbeiten und Sammlungen (Clarifications and Collections)*—and coincides with the failure of the form: "If nature rules the innumerable peculiarities, then it gives form in a normal manner, determining and conditioning; phenomena instead become abnormal when the particularities become overwhelming and stand out in an arbitrary and seemingly random way."[25]

So to speak, the particulars are leaving the stage—sometimes literally. This is testified, for instance, by a famous letter to Goethe in which Schiller—whilst composing *Wallenstein*—wonders how to get rid of all those *Nebedingen*, all those marginal elements that embarrass it.[26] As is known, Schiller solves this problem of the staging of great masses (like an army) by rereading Shakespeare's Roman plays and adopting the Bard's metonymical approach. Think for instance of *Julius Caesar*, where a scene of attempted lynching by a group of Roman citizens against an alleged conspirator becomes the icon of the mood of the Roman masses.

About seventy years later, Ernst Haeckel complained, on a totally different level, about a similar trend to focus on particulars, to lose the type, to nominalism (one could say). In this case what are missing are properly the principles of morphology as the law governing organic becoming, which is not limited to the consideration of the individual being. In the premise to his *Generelle Morphologie der Organismen*, Haeckel notes a sort of diffuse and somewhat uncontrollable morphological anarchy: "Today the thinking consideration of organic forms decreases in fact year after year in inverse proportion to the increase in thoughtless production of raw materials."[27]

Haeckel also stresses that the ideal of a purely descriptive science is essentially impractical and notes that, at the level of morphology, there no longer is the "coordination of the different branches of science of nature"[28] that had instead paid off, for example, in the physiological context. For Haeckel this leads to a sort of anarchy *in morphologicis* after Johannes Muller's death.[29] On the other hand, sciences got lost in exasperated specialism, and this holds especially for morphologism.[30] To pursue the matter from a methodological point of view, the outcome is this: even adding up all the forms to the point of reaching their exhaustive inventory, we would not achieve anything, and we will never be able to achieve "the foundation of a scientific doctrine of forms."[31]

There is no doubt that this is the outset of a nominalistic trend: in the absence of typological models, individual elements are combined and compared with each other. And nominalism goes hand in hand with aestheticization. The principle of affinity in the order of vision turns the images of nature into motifs, as evidenced by Haeckel's influence on the *Jugendstil*.[32] This aestheticization does not concern only morphology. That's what Nietzsche himself learned at his own expense. The young classical philologist noticed precisely this: that the incipient nominalism of scientific research constituted the premise of an aesthetistic betrayal of ancient Greek thought. Not surprisingly, in a letter dating back to when he was a student of classical philology at the University of Leipzig, Nietzsche wrote to his friend Erwin Rohde:

> To see again from close at hand the setting brood of the philologists of our time, and every day having to observe all their moleish pullulating, the baggy cheeks and the blind eyes, their joy at capturing worms and their indifference to the true problems, the urgent problems of life—not only the young ones doing it, but also the old, full-grown ones—all this makes me see more and more clearly that the two of us, if this is to be our only means of remaining true to the spirit in us, shall not go our way in life without a variety of offences and intrigues.[33]

In Nietzsche's later thought, ancient science has lost that unity—found in the ideal/philosophical side and in the real/historical one—that he spoke of in the Basilean lecture *Homer and Classical Philology*, and this produces exactly the kind of effect Nietzsche complains about, for which the two trends are taking different paths and the particular proliferates aimlessly. There are now only incomparable individualities that, in their essentiality, in their uniqueness, touch on the ineffable. Precisely because they lack an inner connection, they offer themselves to the estranged gaze of the aesthetic contemplator.

The point is to find again a living connection that surpasses the irreducibility of the single life, and this is also Dilthey's problem in the building of the human sciences. Those are the sciences of the individual and therefore—we can now add on the basis of the above considerations—they derive from nominalism, which constitutes one of the dominant traits of the *Moderne*, of self-conscious modernity, and they profit from it.

Here one can see a glimpse of a particularly significant trend in this context: that to profit from entropy as one of the main leitmotifs of the *Moderne*, not only in art (as we have seen in the previous chapter and as we see better later). In fact, human sciences have to universalize the particular, endowing it with a universal connection, thus oscillating between individuality and structure.[34] The task at this point is to organize autotelic bodies, self-centering units whose structure, from this point of view, is similar to that of the artwork. To borrow Count Yorck's criticism of Dilthey, they thus offer themselves to the aesthetistic gaze of memory:

> Historical life is productive. It constantly creates goods and things of value and all concepts about them are reflections of this activity.
>
> Objects of value and goods in the mind-constructed world are created by individuals, communities and cultural systems in which the individuals cooperate. [. . .] This creative activity [. . .] occurs in individuals, communities, cultural systems and nations and becomes conscious of itself in the human studies.
>
> In accordance with the structural system, every mental unit has its centre within itself. Like the individual every cultural system, every community has its own focal point. In it, a conception of reality, valuation and the attainment of goals are linked into a whole.
>
> [. . .] A different form of unity arises from the fact that every historical unit has its own centre. Individuals, cultural systems or communities which are contemporaneous and constantly interacting, communicate with each other and thus supplement their own lives with that of others; nations are often relatively self-contained and, because of this, have their own horizons; but, if I now consider the period of the Middle Ages, I find its horizon to be different from that of previous periods. Even where the results of these periods persist they are assimilated into the system of the medieval world

which has a *closed horizon*. Thus an *epoch* is *centred on itself in a new sense*. The common practices of an epoch become the norm for the activities of individuals who live in it. [. . .] Thus every action, every thought, every common activity, in short, every part of this historical whole, has its significance through its relationship to the whole of the epoch or Age. [. . .] We must see the historical world as a whole, this whole as a system of interactions, and this system of interactions as a source of objects of value and purposes (that is as creative). We must understand this whole from within itself and its values and purposes as centred in Ages or epochs of universal history.[35]

Here what automatically comes back to the fore is the ancient Aristotelian connection between history and poetry, which is one of the main threads of these analyses:

Another kind of connection prevails in works which, separated from their authors, have their own life and are a law unto themselves. Before we arrive at the system of interactions in which they originated we must grasp the connections which are there in the completed work. The logical connections which link legal principles into a code of law emerge in understanding. If we read one of Shakespeare's comedies we find the component parts of an event not only temporally and causally linked but elevated into unity according to the laws of poetical composition; this unity lifts the beginning and the end out of the causal chain and links its parts in a whole.[36]

The causal chain produced here is therefore self-centered and its internal articulations, as regards their underlying constraints, refer to the work of art conceived as an organicistic model of Romantic derivation—a model of closed and coherent unity that underpins those thoughts. It is similar to an organism—a teleological unity referring to the great tradition of the late eighteenth-century theory of novel, from von Blankenburg to Friedrich Schlegel. The task is indeed to awaken that unity of life that the causality and the invasiveness of the particular seem to numb and lead to a pure succession of events lacking an inner connection.[37]

From this perspective, indeed, the novel is not only redemptive *for* the particular but also liberating *from* the particular—from the particularity of a life that is thus freed from the casual, accidental, and fundamentally pathological links that weave together the events that make it up. The point is indeed to awaken the autotelic unity, endowed with its own intrinsic end, on which rests the structure of meaning. From the point of view of late eighteenth-century and Romantic theory of the novel, as well as from the standpoint of the nascent sciences of the spirit, life is the syntagma of the challenge that is embodied in the nominalistic vocation of the modern, well represented by the equally modern aesthetic consciousness. For the latter, life experiences and artistic forms represent the modes of an unrepeatable and—upon closer look—irredeemable uniqueness that (being devoid of connections and therefore of a finality), risks remaining inert, meaningless matter. Both the *Erlebnis* (Dilthey's lived experience) and the works born under the sign of the autonomy of art, in fact, are defined based on their separateness—on their escaping any further contextualization.

On both fronts, the issue concerns the form and the quality of the form proposed here. Upon closer inspection, the form established here is closed off and ends up failing, faced with the variety of life it should express. Let me explain. The success of the work, for Dilthey, is realized in the risky passage from experience to form, and this aspect is what shows us the affinities and analogies between the construction of the world and the creation of an artwork.[38] This is all the more evident if one analyzes the way in which, in *The Rise of Hermeneutics*, Dilthey appropriates the old formula that one should understand an author better than he understands himself—which refers to the ever-in-the-making unity of form and content, actualized by the artist in an unconscious way and recognized by the interpreter:

> The rule "understand an author better than he understands himself" also yields the solution to the problem concerning the idea of a poem. It exists (not as abstract thought, quite the opposite) in the sense of an unconscious connection, acting in organizing the work and understandable in its internal form; a poet doesn't use it, and does not become in any way conscious of it; the interpreter puts it in evidence. And this is perhaps the greatest triumph of hermeneutics.[39]

In this context, the problem of *another* form appears. What is outlined here is an incomplete experience of the form that—despite having to do with life in its mobile and uncertain character—is unable to push its limits forward. Hence the necessity—if not yet the idea—of a dynamic form: it is a sort of ideal prelude constituting a very complex fabric, which covers an extremely varied landscape, an observatory which contemplates for example—as we have seen—the rise of the human sciences and that of aesthetic consciousness.

Spengler and Beyond

With Spengler we witness that failure of the form that I wrote about above. This is what can be deduced from the *Decline of the West*, which can rightly be considered a late *summa* of morphological knowledge as well as a prelude to its final decline.[40] In this book one can find the most extreme offshoot of that knowledge of description that was proposed in the name of Goethe and that will come to crash—at least symbolically—with the Heideggerian turn and the meditation on a being that is not the being of the entity.[41] With this, the question about the identities and correspondences between living forms is passed over in favor of the search of a truth that is its prelude; this is the definite end of that approach to the universe—understood as a living, non-objectifiable, whole—which is based on the analogy.

This is instead the background of Spengler's project, thus revealing its intrinsically aesthetic nature. On this basis Spengler avoids dealing with art in the sense of autonomous art or aesthetic art, but, on the other hand, he tends to adopt an aesthetic perspective through the whole of his treatise. This is what he sets out to implement theoretically from the very start:

> Present-day historians think they are doing a work of supererogation in bringing in religious and social, or still more art-history, details to "illustrate" the political sense of an epoch. But the decisive factor—decisive, that is, in so far as visible history is the expression, sign and embodiment of soul—they forget. I have not hitherto found one who has carefully considered the morphological relationship that inwardly binds together the expression-forms of all branches of a Culture, who has gone beyond politics to grasp the ultimate and fundamental ideas of Greeks, Arabians, Indians and Westerners in mathematics, the meaning of their early ornamentation, the basic forms of their architecture, philosophies, dramas and lyrics, their choice and development of great arts, the detail of their craftsmanship and choice of materials—let alone appreciated the decisive importance of these matters for the form-problems of history. Who amongst them realises that between the Differential Calculus and the dynastic principle of

politics in the age of Louis XIV, between the Classical city-state and the Euclidean geometry, between the space-perspective of Western oil-painting and the conquest of space by railroad, telephone and long-range weapon, between contrapuntal music and credit econom-ics, there are deep uniformities? Yet, viewed from this morphological standpoint, even the humdrum facts of politics assume a symbolic and even a metaphysical character, and—what has perhaps been impossible hitherto—things such as the Egyptian administrative sys-tem, the Classical coinage, analytical geometry, the cheque, the Suez Canal, the book-printing of the Chinese, the Prussian Army, and the Roman road-engineering can, as symbols, be made uniformly under-standable and appreciable.[42]

What is outlined, from the historical-philosophical point of view, is a fundamental line: the ultimate development of a perspective that sees the idea of morphology as the unifying motif of knowledge. Spengler's attempt, even if it was destined to fail shortly afterwards, was able to arouse an immense appeal in his time and had wide resonance.[43] This is the extreme rise of morpholog-ical knowledge in its Goethean, but also romantic, appearance according to which knowledge referring to the living is analogical in nature and opposed to physical-mathematical knowledge, which indeed is directed to dead forms: "The means whereby to identify dead forms is Mathematical Law. The means whereby to understand living forms is Analogy. By these means we are enabled to distinguish polarity and periodicity in the world."[44]

To understand the uniqueness of this knowledge, it is necessary to empha-size that it is directed to the relationships; so we are dealing with a perspective that, by highlighting the vital connections of the universe, describes it and sees contemplating consideration (what Goethe called "*Betrachtung*") as an appropri-ate way to interpret it. We are hereby referred to a kind of cosmic artistry accord-ing to which the world should not be interpreted *a parte subjecti*, but according to an immanent gaze, following the intertwining of relationships specified—so to speak—expressively, with the production of symbols. Objectivity and expres-sion become indistinguishable in this framework and are functional to each other in a two-way relationship that is gathered around the notion of symbol. In its Goethean ancestry the symbol refers to the reason for stagnation in the flow of time: to that perspective that identifies the timeless in becoming.[45]

Therefore, this is a purely aesthetic specification that, so to speak, lies in historical development and exposes its fundamental continuum and its periodicity, to use the words of Spengler, without which discontinuity itself would not even be perceived. That is, it would get lost in that atomistic disintegration that—according to what I have attempted to show—produces the path of one of the great forerunners of Spengler—namely, Nietzsche. Besides, it is only in this framework that Spengler's consideration of aesthetics proper can take place. In fact, it acquires its full meaning only insofar as one emphasizes its metaphysical and therefore meta-artistic scope, which is connected, in particular, to the concept of symbol. Art constantly expresses, in this context, the reason for the timeless dimension that flows through time, thus establishing that intersection of time and eternity that structures meaning realizing the impossible—that is, giving stability to becoming, and constancy to caducity.

In this framework, aesthetic consciousness is totally relativized and therefore abolished precisely as it claims to establish itself autonomously. Thus, in Spengler's aesthetic consideration, one finds a singular and interesting *pas des deux*: on the one hand there is the systematic consideration of the arts just as in the great nineteenth-century systems. However, this happens in a context that tends to relativize the significance and scope of the philosophy of art as corresponding, in terms of philosophical systems, to aesthetic consciousness. From this perspective, Spengler's aesthetics, in its dual motivation, constitutes a strange *monstrum,* which, on the one hand, reproduces the categories of classical German aesthetics, from the system of arts to the ancient/modern distinction while, on the other hand, canceling what is properly the core generating such a conceptual scheme: the autonomy of aesthetic consciousness. All this becomes particularly evident in the fourth chapter of the first part of *The Decline of the West.*

However, one should remember that the consideration of art runs through the whole book; the call between the different spheres of being and culture has a vastly superior power to that of their distinction. In particular here applies the dramatic contrast between Faustian and Greek culture, where each of the two imposes its own coinage in all its forms. And while the latter bears the sign of limits and finitude, form and balance, Faustian culture shows the mark of infinity and a *dynamis* that drives it towards the unlimited. The morphology of history, from this point of view, believes that every civilization must be understood as a totality, and that this totality is devoted to the realization of its own inner destiny. It's a single soul that covers an entire civilization and provides its own coinage, so this culture is revealed to itself through its manifestations:

It follows from the meaning that we have attached to the Culture as a prime phenomenon and to destiny as the organic logic of existence, that each Culture must necessarily possess its own destiny-idea. Indeed, this conclusion is implicit from the first in the feeling that every great Culture is nothing but the actualizing and form of a single, singularly-constituted (*einzigartig*) soul.[46]

Every civilization, from this point of view, represents a symbolic expression whose components are correlated by the law of analogy. Spengler especially looks to the Faustian world, derived from joining modernity and Christianity, in an apologetic way: it is the only world that can have knowledge of the idea of free will, destiny, and future.[47] Transcendence awakens freedom; and it is precisely the rise of freedom that gives chance (and not necessity) a decisive meaning. In this framework, though, chance tends to turn into destiny—or rather, destiny finds its own wellspring in chance, in line with the great Shakespearean dramas, especially *Macbeth*.

As can be seen, art is here the symptom—or better, the symbol, of a civilization and, thus, it escapes a purely aesthetic goal and takes on a symbolic-expressive meaning. Of course, in this context, one may wonder whether the importance given to art, considering the epistemological value regarding the knowledge of a world does not end up undermining meaning from the opposite point of view, as for its possibility to express a peculiar efficaciousness on the world itself. Even prescinding from this problem, it is interesting to note how this Faustian—and therefore Christian—constant of modernity in its aspiration to infinity meets a sort of gothic revival that, paradoxically, brings Spengler close to an author such as Ernst Bloch, who is seemingly ideologically and philosophically far from him. For both—under the name of an implicit or explicit Hegelianism—modernity is the product of Christianity, and this means that the gothic style is its adequate icon as opposed to classical measure.[48] From this perspective, Christianity as the background of Faustian culture is responsible for the intimate dynamis of modernity reflected in the gothic.

In this context it is necessary to introduce—albeit en passant—a statement that does not directly affect the texts in question but that allows us, thanks to a kind of short circuit, to go to the heart of the matter. Upon closer inspection, the antithesis between dynamis and stasis, which is introduced by Spengler (on the basis of a very noble influence in a Romantic and idealistic context), should not be thought of in accordance only with the juxtaposition of ancient and modern, or pure monotheism and polytheism. This is the limit of all of Spengler's reflection. In fact, it is not enough to dwell on the historical-temporal alternative without fully grasping the formal models to which it refers us. For Spengler, the Greek *stasis*—where the divine, in its multiple character, takes on a predicative meaning, designating a sphere of being (e.g., Aphrodite means beauty)—contrasts with modern *dynamis*, which concerns instead a God who is not only one but trine.

Let me explain better (and go beyond Spengler): as Jürgen Moltmann rightly noted, in this latter case the divine does not think of itself and should not be thought of as a unity that becomes a triad (and therefore polytheistic), but the other way round—it is a triad that becomes one.[49] This does not imply that the direction is solely the one disclosed by Moltmann, which is that of a historical and eschatological articulation of trinity: it also, and equally, holds true that an intradivine temporality makes divine substance into a subject, thereby returning eternity to historicity in the sign of the modern. In this sense, intradivine temporality is decisive when thinking about modernity, and the latter turns out to be here no longer an element derived by comparison with ancient times, but rather something original. Thus, modernity—with its intimate *dynamis*—does not derive from a more or less traumatic detachment from ancient thought, but from another foundation that actually makes it incomparable to ancient thought itself.

This is a model of divinity that takes time not as a reason for the decadence of the form, but rather considers it in its intimate *dynamis*. There is nothing less classical than the idea of a divinity that moves across its figures, increasing its being in the guise of its multiple semblances, contrary to what happens in ancient Greece where being doesn't continuously grow by taking on different shapes. It might be possible here to outline a history of the metamorphosis that only in modernity can acquire a positive value—contrary to what happens in antiquity, where it is seen as deceit or punishment (one that may fall on those who, like Arachne, have broken the balance between gods and mortals).[50] Only on this basis is it possible to grasp the deep reasons of the end of morphological reason, which I have addressed in these pages. This phenomenon depends on an energetic and dynamic transformation of the form, which isn't entirely grasped by Spengler. It is a morphological innovation that questions the ancient and classic models founded on the ideal of formal stability, and does so up until the extreme measure of losing oneself to find oneself again that is signified by the *kénosis*: God's lowering himself as Christ, who dies on the cross.[51] Here the energetic "collapse" represented by death becomes the principle of a new superior formal dynamic.

Also in the light of these considerations, Spengler's position is particularly significant: it reveals its greatness but also its limits, related to a view that is still affected (albeit by antithesis) by a morphological vision indebted to antiquity, also as for its conception of modernity.

Apollo vs. Faust

To conclude, in the light of these considerations, let's go back to *The Decline of the West*:

The Faustian and the Apollinian images of the soul are in blunt opposition. Once more all the old contrasts crop up. In the Apollinian we have, so to call it, the *soul-body*, in the Faustian the *soul-space*, as the imagination-unit. The body possesses parts, while the space is the scene of processes. Classical man conceives of his inner world plastically. Even Homer's idiom betrays it; echoing, we may well believe, immemorial temple-traditions, he shows us, for instance, the dead in Hades as well-recognizable copies of the bodies that had been. The Pre-Socratic philosophy, with its three well-ordered parts *logistikon*, *epithymetikon*, *thymoeides*, suggests at once the Laocoon group. In our case the impress is a musical one; the sonata of the inner life has the will as first subject, thought and feeling as themes of the second subject; the movement is bound by the strict rules of a spiritual counterpoint, and psychology's business is to discover this counterpoint. The simplest elements fall into antithesis like Classical and Western numbers—on the one hand magnitudes, on the other spiritual relations—and the *spiritual static* of Apollinian existence, the stereometric ideal of *sophrosyne* and *atharaxia* stands opposed to the *soul-dynamic* of Faustian.[52]

The whole of Spengler's aesthetics and perspective could well be inserted in this framework, so intimately related to the Faustian ideal and to what—from a Hegelian standpoint—could be defined as Romantic art (understood as the art born under Christianity). So, what prevails in Christian art is becoming as opposed to being and history as opposed to nature. Overcoming nature, art condemns itself to its own mortality. The triumph of art is also its very end. The framework outlined by Goethe's great pupil—as can be seen—is entirely Hegelian. Art dies because it has lost its sensible resources.[53]

Should we trace all of this back to the main thesis of this book, albeit too brusquely perhaps? By transcending nature, artistic beauty decays in its highest vocation and tends to annihilate itself. Inadvertently indebted to classicity, Spengler melancholically writes in this regard:

All art is mortal, not merely the individual artifacts but the arts themselves. One day the last portrait of Rembrandt and the last bar of Mozart will have ceased to be—though possibly a coloured canvas and a sheet of notes may remain—because the last eye and the last ear accessible to their message will have gone.[54]

Encountering the mortality that belongs to it, art rediscovers its symbolic quality, which nevertheless is mortified. It undoubtedly renews its ability to illuminate the macrocosmos from the viewpoint of the aesthetic microcosmos.[55] But the latter, by now, has narrowed its borders: it represents history and no longer the cosmos as a whole. Art thus takes on a peculiarly expressive and relativistic dimension. In other words, it gives voice to a culture and not to truth.

Getting increasingly closer to the world that it is an expression of, it becomes mass art. Against mass art, whose premise lies in the Enlightenment, modern art proper—of which painting is the most significant example—tends to steer away from common understanding in favor of a shared fruition limited to small circles. In this context, space becomes a mode of interiority. Modern, gothic-Faustian art is therefore antirealistic, and its antirealism constitutes the icon of the "culture against civilization":[56] the hyperbole of an aesthetic modernity that turns against its own historical outcome. From this point of view Spengler takes a paradoxical attitude that, nevertheless, is very consistent: in the name of a modern Faustian ideal, he questions both antiquity and contemporaneity.

This transformation of art, in the end, produces its very disappearance. In this regard, Spengler states that Faustian art is also destined to end, as happens to every art with an almost biological destiny that makes it go through the phases of youth, maturity and old age.[57] The description of the crisis of a civilization reveals an unquestionably Nietzschean influence here: such a crisis, in fact, is mainly related to the form. The symptoms of decadence, showing that the end is near, are the same: the tendency to boundlessness and the trend towards formal dissolution. Spengler can thus say that Nietzsche's criticism of Wagner at the time is the same that could be addressed today to Manet. For Spengler, impressionism (in music or painting) and the propensity to formal minutia approximate very different artists. That's why a work such as *Tristan and Isolde* is the last example of sublime Faustian art, followed by an inevitable decadence whose final outcome is the relapse into naturalism of which—for Spengler—Manet and impressionism are the modern representatives.

If we take Spengler's diagnosis seriously, this is the way the art of sublime yearning goes hand in hand with a relapse into naturalism (another symptom of artistic decadence): thus this is a sort of vicious circle with no way out. On this basis it cannot but become clear that the only way to prevent this failure is to avoid the alternative as it was configured above. It also means addressing the twentieth century as a philosophical problem. To put it in other terms, this means going in the direction of another cognition of the form: a direction that radicalizes Spengler's antinaturalism up to leaving it behind, going beyond representation and the relation between the image and its object. This also allows one to grasp more adequately the link between early Christianity and aesthetic modernity. Abstraction marks a new beginning independent of the reference (be it positive or negative) to nature. This consequently also produces the decline of representation. But what has to be investigated are the modalities of this decline. With Spengler—but not only—begins a singular journey in which the Faustian sublime intertwines with a spiritual, hypernaturalistic inclination of art.

Chapter III

From Modernity to the Avant-Garde

The Gothic Style and the Avant-Garde

In order to really understand the developments of the issue at hand, it is necessary to proceed backwards: from Goethe to German expressionism and to authors such as Spengler (which I have already dealt with) and then to thinkers who were even more closely related to artistic avant-garde, such as Bloch and Worringer. Paradoxically, to explore the bond between beauty and the twentieth century, one must go 140 years back in time and, starting from German expressionism, turn once again to Goethe, in particular to his strategically dense essay "On German Architecture" (1773). In this essay the Gothic style (and its revival) fully reveals its strategic and political importance, which cannot be eluded even when dealing with expressionism.

As we see, the national German theme is always present, from Goethe to its acme in Worringer and in the *Blauer Reiter*. As it had been for his master Herder in *Von deutscher Art und Kunst*,[1] the German theme is for Goethe an anticlassical one: it is not merely national, but universal. Therefore, an anticlassical strategy spreads which is tightly connected to the Gothic soul, a soul that questions gravity and, at the expense of its own stability, challenges the mutual exclusivity of internal and external, typical of Vitruvius's primitive hut. This strategy turns towards the architectural paradox, towards a challenge to statics. It is precisely in those terms that Goethe praises Erwin von Steinbach, the architect who designed the Strasbourg cathedral: "To your teaching, noble genius, I owe thanks that I did not faint and sink before your heights and depths, but that into my soul flowed a drop of that calm rapture of the mighty soul which could look on this creation, and like God say: It is good!"[2]

That the matter was of a political and strategic nature is testified to by that germanicity that is attributed to the Gothic flamboyant of French descent introduced into the German cultural heritage. And in this case germanicity is a matter of style; it is the ideal of a new style which pervades the Nordic world in contrast to the classical one, whose icon is the Vitruvian hut, drawn by the perimeter of the beams upon which another beam is transversally collocated; this outlines the hut and completes it in its structure, which delimits the boundaries of internal and external and, so to speak, invents them.

The Gothic style seems precisely to exclude this horizontal dimension of the internal/external exchange, in order to suggest a vertical organization of space. Thus, the classical balance of forces as they were exemplarily proposed by Winckelmann's description of the *Laocoon*, are set against an airy aspiration that, at least ideally, can never find a keystone in which to gather its forces. One could say that, in the Gothic style, structure conflicts with its own formal model; the keystone in which the drives and counterdrives gather, thus creating a paradoxical balance, is in fact a betrayal of the ideal of the form that seeks transcendence.

Hence the outline of the connection between form and expression, which is the main thread running through the considerations to follow in this section. As said above, the formal ideal appears to conflict with its own architectural structure; this means that here the form conflicts with its very own formal arrangement. In other words, this is a form whose components do not tend to a synergic organization: they cannot virtuously exploit their energies so as to produce balance. This is a formal ideal characterized by a remarkable paradoxicality, bound to contradict and negate itself, because its aim is essentially impossible: to reach infinity.

One could anticipate that what is being prepared here is the path towards the formulation of Goethe's symbol as a form capable of harboring an infinite content. But there is much more than that. In fact, this form tends towards entropy: it is an open form that seems bound to lose rather than to contain, to lose what is inside it but also to lose itself. In realizing its ideal, it inevitably strives beyond itself, and opens itself up to the extreme limit of its very own capacity. But, as a result of this opening, its components, struggling for an impossible synergy, instead of meeting as directional lines, may end up separating from each other at the end of their path, just like fireworks.

This alternative is definitely epochal, and will also be revived a little later by Schiller in "The Horae." Further evidence of its momentousness can be found in Bendavid's essay "Über griechische und gotische Baukunst," which outlines the historical, much more than stylistical, antithesis that began to be developed in Goethe's essay.[3] This antithesis is a fundamental one and will tend to be normalized in the future. However, what's at stake here is not merely the opposition between "closed form" and "open form" (to use Wölfflin's formulation, which I deal with again later).[4] There is another fundamental element that emerges from Goethe's considerations and that will persist as a theme of major significance till the very end of the journey: the centrality of decorative art. Goethe states that his first impression of the Strasbourg cathedral was a negative one because of the overabundance of ornament: "Quite buried in ornamentation! Consequently I had an aversion to seeing it, such as I would have before a malformed bristling monster."[5]

This inclination towards the ornament—understood as something autonomous and independent from the structure it relies on and enriches, as something that does not abide by the logic of the supplement (as Derrida said in *The Truth in Painting*)[6]—is one of the common elements to all the interpretations of the Gothic style, and one of great importance. As I explain later, the ornament, as a primeval and original element, is the theme that makes it possible to fully explore the reception of the Gothic style and, conversely, to observe the temptation to classicize itself, which it repeatedly falls into.

Indeed, the classicization of the Gothic style occurs more than once, and coincides with its being proposed as a style, similarly to what happened with classicism (for example, with its reception from a Neopalladian perspective). The dividing line between ancient and modern here turns into another divide, maybe even more influential than the previous one: the one that separates style, with its modular and serial nature, from the nominalistic vocation of aesthetic modernity, which aims at considering the artistic work starting only from itself: the artistic work finds a hyperbolic confirmation in the autonomy of the ornament. More in general, this means that the modern style is aesthetically destined to see the work of art as an incomparable event. But if it really is an incomparable event, what there is time after time is not a work of art, and not even a form of art; it is art as a whole, which each time is materialized in this or that work of art. Anticipating the sometimes adventurous journey of this chapter, which proceeds from the Gothic style to expressionist avant-garde and from the latter to Benedetto Croce's aesthetics, a work of art is vocationally a total work of art on the basis of the vocation of aesthetic modernity, which dissolves every discipline or norm that lies outside the artwork itself and transcends it with an authority that is perceived as dominating and unacceptable.

Before reaching the articulate formulation of the thesis stated above, however, it is necessary to go back to the issue of the Gothic revival and to underline that one cannot talk about the Gothic style in late-seventeenth-century
German culture without dwelling on Willhelm Heinrich Wackenroder, who
inaugurated the revival of the Gothic style in a spirit of a possible equilibrium
with classicism. In Wackenroder's analysis, the Gothic style and classical style
take shape in the antithesis between Dürer and Raphael, understood as two
(also anthropological) roots of European culture: the Greek and the Jewish-
Christian traditions. As is well known, Wackenroder evokes medieval Nuremberg; and it must be noticed that this evocation has historical and political
implications of primary importance. In his eyes, Nuremberg is the city whose
thousand spires evoke a political universe resembling an organism or an artwork. Integrating the social, political, and religious universe, and proudly displaying the continuity between art and handicraft, the organization of the
medieval cosmos refers to an ideal of community whose utopian model lies in
the artwork and in beauty.

From this viewpoint, Wackenroder's Middle Ages become similar to
Greece from a classicistic viewpoint: a universe that conjoins *ethos* and *polis*.
Discussing Dürer's world in "A Portrayal of how the early German painters
lived: in which are introduced as examples Albrecht Dürer along with his
father Albrecht Dürer the Elder," Wackenroder writes: "From such examples
one will perceive that where art and religion unite, the most beautiful river of
life flows forth out of the converging streams."[7] Thanks to this classicistic view
of beauty, which is nevertheless attributed to the Gothic style, it is possible to
reach a reconciliation between the Christian-modern world that developed
under Christianity and the ancient world—a reconciliation that symbolically
takes place in the association between Dürer and Raphael, as well as Germany
and Italy, which was recovered by the group of Romantic painters, called the
"Nazarenes," who worked in Rome in the early nineteenth century. Dürer's
self-portrait with "Nazarene" hair was one of their figurative points of reference that paved the way to the modern aestheticization of religion.

Going back to Wackenroder, the reconciliation mentioned above, however, raises serious questions. On the one hand, behind the image of medieval Nuremberg, its high spires and the quiet life of the corporations, one
finds again the classicistic idea of beauty as perfect organic harmony. Actually,
this could arouse suspicion about the very ideal, about a possible totalitarian
nature of beauty in which the internal differences and articulations are com-
pressed, thus hindering the free interactions between the components. This is

even more surprising as it happens within the Gothic style—the artistic ideal that does not mainly aim at the integration of its components, but rather at their disarticulation. And there's more. Something even subtler is happening here. The Gothic style is shifting towards the classical, and in doing so it embraces a paradoxical fate: it becomes an actual style, presenting itself no longer as an event—that of its own impossible edification—but as a module. This implies that it can be considered an indefinitely replicable model, just like the classical style. Wackenroder's Middle Ages thus become very similar to classical Greece: as I have already said, they both recall a continuity of ethos and polis in which religion is the skeleton of the community. In this case the difference between the pure and simple faith of the medieval city—shared by all the people regardless of their social status—and the cult of the ancient gods is actually not that relevant: it concerns only customs, not deeply rooted mentalities.

It might be useful to notice that all of this happens again in the second part of the nineteenth century, when William Morris more widely reintroduces the Gothic as a style. As is well known, Morris sought to combine the romantic Middle Ages and socialism; this unprecedented union increasingly reinforced the role of the Gothic style as the ultimate modern model—the new style. Morris's Middle Ages—like Wackenroder's—appears as a universe characterized by a strong social integration based on corporations, where there is no capitalistic division of labor and work is still a source of pleasure. It is an apology of craftsmanship and popular art.

> Why has civilized society in all that relates to the beauty of man's handiwork degenerated from the times of the barbarous, superstitious, unpeaceful Middle Ages? [. . .] Popular art, that is, the art which is made by the cooperation of many minds and hands varying in kind and degree of talent, but all doing their part in due subordination to a great whole, without anyone losing his individuality—the loss of such an art is surely great, nay, inestimable. [. . .] For I say unhesitatingly that the intelligent work which produced real art was pleasant to do, was human work, not over burdensome and degrading; whereas the unintelligent work, which produces sham art, is irksome to do, it is unhuman work, burdensome and degrading: so that it is but right and proper that it should turn out nothing but ugly things. And the immediate cause of this degrading labour which oppresses so large a part of our people is the system of the organisation of labour,

which is the chief instrument of the great power of modern Europe, competitive commerce. That system has quite changed the way of working in all matters that can be considered as art, and the change is a much greater one than people know of or think of. In times past these handicrafts were done on a small, almost a domestic, scale by knots of workmen who mostly belonged to organized gilds, and were taught their work soundly, however limited their education was in other respects. [8]

Morris's main aim is to remedy to the anarchic development produced by the capitalistic economy, not only in reference to the organization of labor, but also to city planning. This can be achieved through leveling out the differences and achieving a new stylistic unity whose sole common denominator is the Gothic style. As in Wackenroder, so in Morris the emerging idea of beauty is that of a "reconciliation" (hidden under political intentions and concerns) uniting the several spheres of life. Therefore here one finds once more the continuity between ethos and polis—the main thread of romantic beauty. Though in a softer form, mitigated by the democratic ambitions of this thinking, in this case an inclination to a totalitarianism of beauty is outlined; this translates into the ideal of the Gothic style, which reached the circle of pre-Raphaelite painters as well, some of whom were close to Morris. This is a stylistic unity that harmonically shapes a world as a whole:

> Under all these conditions I should certainly get the last want accomplished which I am now going to name. I want all the works of man's hand to be beautiful, rising in fair and honourable gradation from the simplest household goods to the stately public building, adorned with the handiwork of the greatest masters of expression which that real new birth and the dayspring of hope come back will bring forth for us.[9]

The stylistic unity thus coincides with the ideal of beauty in which repeatability and regularity are progressively overshadowing the event-like quality of art. This gives some insight into the fate of the ambiguous Gothic style, which, as has been seen, swings between two temptations—the two conflicting inclinations I have tackled so far. This means that on the one hand the Gothic sublimely strives for infinity, while, on the other hand, tending to assert itself as a style, thus belonging completely to its time. In the latter case the Gothic style—betraying itself—aims at restoring the ancient order of supreme beauty that imposes its forms upon this world, giving up any propensity towards transcendence.

The contradictory vocation of the Gothic style is all the more significant in that it mirrors the contradictory development of aesthetic modernity: the falling apart of style and expression which is dealt with in the following pages. Its stylistic inclination—in a broad sense—which conflicts with its deepest vocation, arises repeatedly and is testified to by the neo-Gothic renaissance of the second half of the nineteenth century, among whose representatives one finds Philipp Webb, an architect close to Morris.

It is interesting to notice that in these circumstances it is precisely Morris's master, John Ruskin, who, contrary to his disciple, gives new life to the inner antinormative, antistylistic character of the Gothic style. In him one finds the same paradoxical nature of the Gothic style as in Goethe. In the chapter "Stones of Venice," dedicated to the *Nature of Gothic*, he writes that the Gothic style could be framed by six categories, which he lists in order of importance:

1. Savageness.
2. Changefulness.
3. Naturalism.
4. Grotesqueness.
5. Rigidity.
6. Redundance.[10]

It is truly significant that here, when the nineteenth-century revival of the Gothic style is at its peak, its original dimension emerges again as it had appeared in Goethe. Here again the inclination of the Gothic style towards savageness and redundance is positively evaluated because of its antistylistic mark, because it stems from Christianity and from its inclination to bring out particularity and individuality. Once again the Gothic style testifies to a deep dissatisfaction: it is characterized by "a magnificent enthusiasm, which feels as if it never could do enough to reach the fullness of its ideal."[11] This shows—as it did in Goethe—some sort of anthropologic soul; it belongs to the history of Northern people and is an essential part of their rough nature and their desire for freedom; instead, it contrasts with the classical soul of Southern people, which tends to a regularity that is almost submission and from which the exuberant redundance of ornamentation is excluded.[12]

The inner deconstructive soul of the Gothic form, which tends to break down into its own components, emerges here once more but then succumbs again to the temptation of presenting itself as a style, as a modern and Christian model in contrast to (but after all in consonance with) the ancient-classical model. The Gothic stylistic uniformity clashes with the most intimate vocation of the Gothic style itself, which is always destructuring itself in order to create, from an original unity, derived forms generated by the components of the main one.

This same path will be taken by the artistic avant-garde and especially the *Blauer Reiter*, which represents that paradoxical event of the Gothic soul disaggregating its components and animating them in their own singularity. This gives rise to an intensification of the single formal elements that develop a new living balance among themselves.

Expressionism and the Gothic Style

Getting straight to the point, it is well known that the almanac of the *Blauer Reiter* develops a system of illustrations which originates from various different traditions: from the recovery of the *Glasbilder*, the glass paintings from Bavaria that owe to Gothic imagination, to the so-called primitive art, and to images that mainly come from the circle of painters of the *Blauer Reiter* or at least syntonic to their taste.[13]

An element that can help to understand this situation can be found precisely in this mixture of different styles, which define a space full of unprecedented combinations or contaminations, where absolute traditions are thus profoundly challenged and deconstructed through the visual analogy between the Gothic style and both primitive art and the avant-garde. All this goes along with a thematization of form, always intended as tension and not as stasis. This is especially evident, for example, in August Macke's essay "Die Masken," full of images that come from the primitive art of Latin America, Easter Island, and New Caledonia. This essay affirms indeed the expressive character of every form of art and also the idea that the form of art flows from a tension that wants to be released:

> Each authentic form of art emerges from a reciprocal interrelation
> of man and the factual materials of the forms of nature, of the art
> forms. [. . .] The flower opens when dawn creeps in. The panther
> ducks down at the sight of its prey, and his power grows as a result of

this view. And from the tension of his strength results the scope of his jump. An art form, a style, emerges from a tension.[14]

Macke also noticed that this expressive tension coincides with a disaggregation of figurative components, which leads to a liberation of constituent elements and volumes. This blows up the idea of a founding tradition while also connecting different traditions. From this viewpoint, Macke can affirm that

> the bronze casts of the inhabitants of Benin (West Africa), discovered not until 1889, the idols of the Easter Islands in the Pacific Ocean, the collar of the chief from Alaska, and the wooden mask from New Caledonia speak the same strong language as the Chimeras on the Paris Notre-Dame Cathedral and the grave stone in Frankfurt Cathedral.[15]

Thanks to this expressive tension, which can even generate unprecedented contaminations, the Gothic soul reveals itself in its completeness as the true soul of modernity. One could say it is precisely in this context that the Gothic "open form" finally reaches abstraction, or better still, it generates abstraction, in that it takes the principle of asymmetry to its extreme peak—which entails scattering the original components and then putting them back together, integrating external elements as well. However, this is not about an objective decomposition of the artwork in the elements that, as far as volume and surface are concerned, define its formal structure. In this regard, the comparison with cubist decomposition naturally arises. In this respect, Macke says: "What is Cubism? It is mostly a conscious desire to restore to painting the knowledge of measure, volume and weight."[16]

According to Macke, within the *Blauer Reiter* the decomposition is far more intense and advanced; as in the Gothic style, it is subjectivity that sets in motion the components, outlining not a stasis, but a dynamic of elements, which involves not only volume, but also color. This dynamic introduces these elements into a movement of "spiritualization." In this regard it is Franz Marc (and no longer Macke) who underlines the great distance of his own poetics from impressionism, but also from cubist decomposition.[17] Of course at this point it is necessary to define the meaning of spiritualization: it coincides with a sort of 'truthful' urge of art that—as is seen more in detail in the following pages—characterizes a large part of contemporary aesthetics. Kandinsky also appeals to the spiritual dimension precisely in the opening of his essay "On the Question of Form," in which he warns that "at the appointed time, necessities become ripe. That is, the creative spirit (which one can designate as the Abstract Spirit) finds an avenue to the soul, later to other souls, and causes a yearning, an inner urge."[18]

According to Kandinsky, an inner spiritual urge pervades the components and makes art go beyond realism, but also beyond abstraction understood as its mere opposite, as a mere absence of representation. In Kandisky's view, great abstraction and great realism are the two poles of a single development and will eventually unite. This path towards a single goal determines an interruption of the path in which abstraction and objectivity never coexist, so that the orders they both represent are shaken. The primacy of realism and/or abstraction is replaced by the primacy of "inner sounds." It is about leading the components, whatever their origin, to such an intensification that a radical change in meaning will take place. Going beyond the realism/abstraction alternative means completely relativizing and finally radically questioning the issue of form in its traditional connotation. In a word, the artwork has its own subjectivity. This question was addressed not only by Kandinsky, but also, and maybe above all, by Paul Klee in his "Creative Confession."

In his essay "On the Question of Form," Kandinsky strongly negates the meaningfulness of investigating whether form is somehow related to the objective world. Its content comes from somewhere else anyway; it is based on inner sounds. From this point of view, what is being overstepped is the very question of form, at least as form *of* something:

> Thus we arrive at the result that pure abstraction also makes use of things which lead their material existence, just as pure realism does. The greatest negation of the objective and its greatest affirmation again receive the sign of equality. And this sign is again justified by the mutually held aim: by the embodying of the same inner resonance.
>
> Here we see that as a matter of principle *it has no significance at all whether real or abstract form is used by the artist.*
>
> *Since both forms are internally equal* the choice must be left to the artist, who must know best himself by which means he can materialize most clearly the content of his art. Abstractly put: *In principle, there is no question of form.*[19]

It is on the basis of similar premises that Klee is able to think of an artwork that overturns the relationship with the object in the contemplative exchange, reflecting on a painting that observes its observers and thus becoming totally autonomous from them. Klee states:

> And every figure, every combination will have its particular constructive expression, every form its face, its physiognomy. The pictures of objects look out at us, serene or severe, tense or relaxed, comforting or forbidding, suffering or smiling. They look out at us in all the contrasts of the physical-physiognomic dimension; they can extend from tragedy to comedy.[20]

This autonomy of the artwork from its interpreter will be the influential model of the twentieth century from now on. Along with it, another principle is overwhelmingly established: that of nonmeaningfulness—the image does not refer to the objective world. This means it is necessary to take a step back: *Zurück zu Goethe*, back to Goethe, back to the beginning of this chapter about Gothic ornamentation, which does not depend—at least from a semantic point of view—on the structure upon which it stands, but rather has an autonomous meaning.

From Goethe to Worringer and Beyond

The ornamentality whose contradictory character upset young Goethe while looking at the Strasbourg cathedral comes back again in the eyes of a philosopher who also was a well-respected theorist of expressionism: Wilhelm Worringer. This kind of ornament has "something more" and so does representation; and it is precisely this "something" that arises with expressionism, according to what Worringer writes in essays such as "Greek Culture and the Gothic," "On the Question of Gothic Monumentality," and "The Late Gothic and Expressionist System of Form."[21]

It is interesting to notice how Worringer, as early as 1916, renews the relationship between the Gothic style and aesthetic modernity: in his view, it relies on the strong bond between medieval spirituality and the features of the German people. Thus the traditional relationship between popular tradition and individual invention—which ran through the whole history of the Gothic style from Wackenroder to Morris and eventually to German expressionism—arises once again. Quite remarkably, Worringer sees the Gothic style as the antithesis not of the Greek-classical style, but rather of its degeneration under the Romans. The Gothic style exemplifies a form that hosts becoming and is not rigid, contrary to the fixity, the *Festigheit* typical of Roman art. Moreover, this fluidity of the Gothic form, which also relates to its elevation and its struggle to find infinity in finitude, is the reason for its constitutive incompleteness; however, incompleteness does not really harm such a form. Precisely because of this ambition to reconcile with infinity, Worringer can also affirm that what is being conceived as "'divine *pride* in stone' can easily become its blasphemous opposite, a 'God *notwithstanding* in stone'"[22]—that is, an arrogant testimony of human hubris that might very well provoke divine wrath.

Worringer also observes that, from this point of view, it is no coincidence that the products of the Gothic style often remain fragmentary. In Worringer's view, the fragmentary nature of Gothic monuments does not depend on only external reasons—such as, for example, the difficulty in finding the money to pay for the realization of such majestic buildings—but also on reasons internal to this form, which is devoted to incompleteness precisely because it longs for infinity. Here emerges one of the paradoxes of Worringer's Gothic, a paradox that looks back to Goethe's considerations and also points towards expressionism: an overtly anti-imitative direction that, however, pursues a semiorganicist ideal. This is the secret of the ornament: the ornament conjoins organism and antinaturalism in a mixture that is theoretically impossible but practically real: in this regard, Gothic art is truly the precursor of expressionism.

> This art does not know any path leading directly to nature—and this is because it lacks the instinctive consonance with nature—for this purpose it turns the thousand lateral paths that lead exclusively through reality into the unique world of solely artistic expression. If you will, it is an abstract grimace of nature that is open in respect of each hyperbole and every expressive strengthening, and yet profoundly significant.
>
> Stylized antinature, a grimace of nature, interwoven with acute ingredients of reality and an abstract expressiveness of the autonomous and lucubrating nature: can one not sense the possibility of dialogue with expressionism here?[23]

This path leads to a more elevated symbology, one that uses the organic to reach a higher level. In this regard, Worringer observes that anatomy—and therefore the organism—plays a role both in expressionism and in Gothic style, but that expressionism has to do with a cosmic organism.[24] Finally, he points out how this process takes place at a time when the style of an epoch, the *Zeitstil*, is reunited to the style of the people, the *Volksstil*. Worringer finds this all the more paradoxical as it happens to cultures that never aimed at a complete development of their components, but at a partial, unilateral one, in line with the most intimate inclinations of the Gothic soul that enhances its own components at the expense of the whole.[25]

Starting from the various Gothic revivals, some cultural physiognomies start to develop that pave the way to German avant-garde. So the Gothic style is actually a thread that runs through extremely significant moments of twentieth-century aesthetics, introducing a 'new' aesthetic ideal, which has been an alternative to the classical one since the very beginning. As Schiller already noted in "On Naive and Sentimental Poetry," modern art relies on a representative distance from its object, and therefore longs for an impossible agnition. It is precisely in the enhanced and painful sensibility towards this distance that one can truly find the essence of the so-called moderne, the aesthetic modernity. Its root lies precisely in the gap between idea and reality. As we have seen, this happens with German Romanticism that—with a sort of satisfied regret—looks behind itself, at beauty, at the classical style as the complete integration of form and content, of idea and reality. These are the circumstances in which the Gothic style finds its peculiar place: it represents the original form of this necessary gap that characterizes the moderne.

So even Spengler—who has already been dealt with in the previous chapter—in his book *The Decline of the West* acknowledges that the "infinite space"—of which the Gothic style is the icon—"is the ideal that the Western soul has always striven to find [. . .] in its world around."[26] The Faustian soul, which is typically modern, is expressed for Spengler by free will, by the tension towards the future, by the look towards destiny as a mystery that recalls the way the Gothic world looks towards infinity.[27] In Spengler's view, the Gothic style thus pervades modern art as a whole, as is shown by poetry and architecture, but also by the tension towards emptiness and the unlimited typical of northern poetry as opposed to Homeric verse.[28] As we have seen, this also frames Spengler's analogy: he compares Catholic faith to an altarpiece and Protestant faith to an oratorio.[29]

This is how style expresses a civilization,[30] voicing its cultural forms that act like a system of communicating vessels connected to each other. The Gothic line thus contains the principle of the infinitesimal;[31] it produces an art that, because of its nonimitative nature, is not accessible to everyone. This is a core point that goes back again to the beginning of this chapter: the ornament.

It is the peak of this journey through the Gothic style: at this point, ornament goes side by side with nonmeaningfulness, in a sort of polemic distance from any imitative ideal of art:

> To that extent, imitation belongs to Time and Direction. [. . .] Ornament, on the contrary, is something taken away from Time: it is pure extension, settled and stable. Whereas an imitation expresses something by *accomplishing itself,* ornament can only do so by presenting itself to the senses as a finished thing. It is Being as such, wholly independent of origin.[32]

Thus the journey through the ornament is the prelude, or better still, the *pendant* of the journey towards abstraction. On the other hand, abstraction stems from a journey that starts within temporality and then moves on to atemporality, where it finds is adequate place.

Even a neo-Marxist thinker as different from Spengler as Ernst Bloch would agree with such statements. In *The Spirit of Utopia* (in the same years and in terms similar to Spengler's), Bloch develops the affinity between the Gothic style and expressionism. Again, the heart of this affinity lies in the concept of ornament. Here again one finds the contrast between dynamis and stasis, which appears as the contrast between Egyptian and Gothic. Taking up Hegel's teaching in a totally original way, Bloch sees in Egyptian art the expression of the principle of a laborious control over materials. The Gothic-Christian yearning flows through the materials, animates them, and permeates them expanding into the surroundings:

> For Egypt remains the notion as well as the fulfillment of complete, uninterrupted shape, of the *meaningful* construction and immanence of stone in general, dictated by the spirit of the material itself, not by stylizing efforts. Only Christian life penetrates the stone in a serious way. In this instance even the *external space* might become Gothic, and the angelic salutation in the gallery of the Church of Lorenx in Nuremberg had been created precisely to celebrate the space where it hangs, to make the space sing and to become the focus, particularly by hanging in the center, of the internal sounding of the church's spatial body.[33]

The warm vitality of the organism evoked by Gothic volutes and developed in the ornament thus conflicts with the principle of Egyptian petrified motionlessness. The organic dimension is moreover the welcoming dimension of the maternal womb, in which internal and external overcome the barriers that divide them, establishing a relationship with each other and building the premises of the world of expression; this brings out the hieroglyphic that conceals the hidden—albeit always present—human figure. Ornament puts humankind into contact with the deep, unconscious layers of the historical being that emerge in the world of expression. This principle is organic and psychic at the same time; however recognizable these forms may be, they do not belong to reality:

> During the *Gothic* period [. . .] the organic, psychical yearning manifested itself truly as ornament. We know the entanglements, the serpentine bodes, the sea horses, the dragon heads bent toward each other in the Nordic lineations. There is nothing that could be compared with this uncanny pathos derived from the vitalization of the inorganic. Therefore, if now there is still any possible salvation behind the rejected, worn-out styles, then it can only happen through the resumption of those almost completely forgotten organic lines. [. . .] The *Gothic* line [. . .] retains the hearth; this line is restless and uncanny like its figures: the bulges, the serpents, the animal heads, the watercourses, a tangled criss-cross and twitching where the amniotic fluid and the incubation heat sit, and the womb of all pains, all lusts, all births, and of all organic images begin to speak. Only the Gothic line carries such a central fire within itself in which the most profound organic and the most profound spiritual essence come to maturity.[34]

This is the origin of a utopian art in which the "ornamentation and signature of the immediate human being" begins to appear.[35] It is a completely new path from which an "irreversible," "mystical nominalism" emerges:[36] this means that every artwork is potentially the whole world of art. According to Bloch, this is the new and eternal essence of art. It is an art that from now on intends to propose itself as a new whole.

Croce: An Enemy of the Avant-Garde?

Summing up what has been said so far, a nominalistic tendency emerges in aesthetics. In other words, art does no longer belong to the philosophic universe of aesthetic categories but presents itself as a redeeming motive, or at least as an absolute event. Art seeks a reunification with life: this is one of the core traits of artistic avant-garde.[37] From Croce to authors very different from him, such as Adorno and Benjamin, the artwork tends more and more to become an event, or at least to put this inclination into practice, trespassing the boundaries of aesthetic conscience and setting aside the historical legacy of aesthetic categories.

The journey through Croce's thought has to start in medias res. First of all, it is essential to observe that Croce's aesthetics, precisely because of its neoclassical character—precisely by praising the beauty that almost fades into pure intuition—ends up going in the opposite direction, destroying not only genres (as is openly stated), but even the borders between arts (if not expressly, at least theoretically). This motion overthrows the definition of art, which will no longer be the single artwork, or will be such only insofar as it represents art as a whole. From this perspective, every artwork is, albeit unconsciously, a total artwork. And this is probably how one should conceive the cosmic scope of the artwork as Croce describes it in works such as "The *Totality* in *Artistic Expression*," *which is analyzed later.*

It is well known that Croce never gave up on his initial fundamental idea that art derives from the union of intuition and expression. This very simple but brilliant idea joins—almost unexpectedly—the two roots of modern aesthetics: that à la Leibnitz and Baumgartner, which aims at defining aesthetic knowledge on the basis of perception, and the one that leads to nineteenth- and twentieth-century philosophy of art. The first pages of *Aesthetic* (1902) are really significant in this respect:

> And yet there is a sure method of distinguishing true intuition, true representation, from that which is inferior to it: the spiritual fact from the mechanical, passive, natural fact. Every true intuition or representation is, also, expression. That which does not objectify itself in expression is not intuition or representation, but sensation and naturality. The spirit does not obtain intuitions, otherwise than by making, forming, expressing. He who separates intuition from expression never succeeds in reuniting them.
>
> *Intuitive activity possesses intuitions to the extent that it expresses them.* [. . .] But be it pictorial, or verbal, or musical, or whatever else it be called, to no intuition can expression be wanting, because it is an inseparable part of intuition.[38]

Here the focus is shifting towards a celebration of form and with it, of beauty, from which it cannot be separated. Croce underlines this shortly after, thus arriving to a crucial point not only of *Aesthetic*, but of all Croce's considerations on the topic:

> In the aesthetic act, the aesthetic activity is not added to the fact of the impressions, but these latter are formed and elaborated by it. The impressions reappear as it were in expression, like water put into a filter, which reappears the same and yet different on the other side. The aesthetic fact, therefore, is form, and nothing but form.[39]

Now, if the aesthetic act is to be intended as a successful union of intuition and expression, which lives off its own self-realization—that is, its formal success—this is the way beauty (truly a key category in Croce's aesthetics) coincides with the success of form. Therefore, beauty is to be understood as successful expression, whereas ugliness as unsuccessful expression.[40]

So the artwork lives fully and completely in its self-realization—following a tendency that Croce will underline in *Poetry*; a tendency that leads to a peculiar hermeneutic conception of the artwork characterized by a strong nominalism—that is, as we have seen, by the inclination to give up on any universal philosophical parameter. Here, too, Croce's reasoning seems to proceed by harmlessly following the routes of common sense; what it truly does, though, is take an absolutely radical route, which heralds the cancellation of all aesthetic categories provided by tradition. As is well known, Croce thinks that the beautiful can be said in a variety of ways and values, with reference to scientific truths or to moral behavior. However, the term "beautiful" pertains par excellence to the sphere of aesthetics, and it designates a successful expression.

> But after all the explanations that have been given, and all danger of misunderstanding being now dissipated, and since, on the other hand, we cannot fail to recognize that the prevailing tendency, alike in current speech and in philosophy, is to limit the meaning of the vocable beautiful altogether to the aesthetic value, we may define beauty as successful expression, or better, as expression and nothing more, because expression, when it is not successful, is not expression.
>
> Consequently, the ugly is unsuccessful expression. The paradox is true, that, in works of art that are failures, the beautiful is present as *unity* and the ugly as *multiplicity*. Thus, with regard to works of

art that are more or less failures, we talk of qualities, that is to say of *those parts of them that are beautiful*. We do not talk thus of perfect works. It is in fact impossible to enumerate their qualities or to designate those parts of them that are beautiful. In them there is complete fusion: they have but one quality. Life circulates in the whole organism: it is not withdrawn into certain parts.

The qualities of works that are failures may be of various degrees. They may even be very great. The beautiful does not possess degrees, for there is no conceiving a more beautiful, that is, an expressive that is more expressive, an adequate that is more than adequate. Ugliness, on the other hand, does possess degrees, from the rather ugly (or almost beautiful) to the extremely ugly. But if the ugly were *complete,* that is to say, without any element of beauty, it would for that very reason cease to be ugly, because in it would be absent the contradiction which is the reason of its existence. The disvalue would become nonvalue; activity would give place to passivity, with which it is not at war, save when there effectively is war.

And because the distinctive consciousness of the beautiful and of the ugly is based on the contrasts and contradictions in which aesthetic activity is developed, it is evident that this consciousness becomes attenuated to the point of disappearing altogether, as we descend from the more complicated to the more simple and to the simplest cases of expression. From this arises the illusion that there are expressions which are neither beautiful nor ugly, those which are obtained without sensible effort and appear easy and natural being so considered.[41]

In the light of these considerations, several central aspects of Croce's thinking become crystal clear. First of all, beauty is a unique category, as opposed to the many forms of ugliness. Thus the unsuccessful has a thousand forms, whereas the successful has only one, and therefore it is pointless (at least from the perspective of aesthetic judgment) to consider the potential variants of an artwork. Secondly, all the variables relating to positive predicates of the artwork, and above all the category of the sublime, cease to exist here, with the consequent monocratic triumph of beauty as a fluent organism that finds no obstacle whatsoever on its way.

As is well known, this is an enormous reconsideration of aesthetic categories, which leaves behind the greatest part of the journey of nineteenth-century philosophy of art. It is a sort of absolute neoclassicism, an unconditioned triumph of beauty, which reduces all the other categories to nothing, leaving aside the historic awareness that had matured in nineteenth-century philosophy of art.[42] For Croce, this redimensioning of aesthetic categories—whose historic awareness goes back to what has been defined as "the age of Goethe"[43]—that is, to those three decades of German culture that end with Hegel's and Goethe's almost simultaneous deaths[44]—implies a true catastrophe, an annulment of a centuries-old tradition, despite the flaunted and almost blasé simplicity of the gesture.

This is one of the most paradoxical passages, and it basically concerns the meaninglessness of the attention to the historical significance of artworks. Due to the union of intuition and expression, temporality relates solely to the occurrence of the artwork with no comparisons; thus the artwork presents itself more and more as an absolute, incomparable event. Therefore it cannot be integrated in a perspective that refers to the philosophy of history, as happened with the majestic constructions of the philosophy of art in the idealistic and Romantic period. Since it is an absolute event, the artwork does not depend on time; its meaning is completely intrinsic to it.[45]

This means that it is essentially impossible to see any progress in art;[46] rather, it is the artwork that continues to impose itself as an absolute event, which cannot be related to what happened before or will happen after. Croce here refuses any model within artistic tradition, which is challenged as such.

> Concepts and models alike have no existence in art, for by proclaiming that every art can be judged only in itself, and has its own model in itself, they have attained to the denial of the existence of objective models of beauty, whether they be intellectual concepts, or ideas suspended in the metaphysical sky.[47]

So time after time, the work of art establishes itself as the totality of art, as a sort of total work of art irrespective of the means it uses, which are irrelevant as regards its authentic finality. This implies, on the one hand, that every artwork (at least potentially) carries in itself all the expressive means of art; on the other hand, that it proposes itself as an occurrence; and this is where its hermeneutic implications are revealed. Every work of art is the realization and clarification of itself.

If the work of art is an occurrence, this is its peculiar historical significance, which does not overlap ex post with its being, but is rather consustantial to it. On this premise is it possible to define the identity between linguistics and aesthetics, where the structural aspect of language—in other words, grammar—results in what would be defined à la Saussure as a single "act of *parole*," whose sense is always new even though the linguistic utterance is the same:

> If Linguistic and Esthetic appear to be two different sciences, this arises from the fact that people think of the former as grammar, or as a mixture between philosophy and grammar, that is, an arbitrary mnemonic scheme. They do not think of it as a rational science and as a pure philosophy of speech. Grammar, or something grammatical, also causes the prejudice in people's minds that the reality of language lies in isolated and combinable words, not in living discourse among expressive organisms, rationally indivisible.[48]

In a similar way, in *La poesia,* Croce states that every poem is occasional poetry.[49] In other words, a poem is an event that makes people aware of its absolute, unique character every time it occurs. From this perspective, albeit remaining far from any form of vitalism, Croce claims the "actuality in becoming" of the artwork. If words live off their occurring, the present is definitely the temporal ecstasy that best suits the work of art, considered an absolute present which borders on eternity:

> Poetry is the language in its genuinity. [. . .] Even in everyday conversation and expression, if one pays attention, one can see how, along its bustling course, words are continuosly renewed and imaginatively invented and poetry—with the most varied tones, severe and sublime, tender, graceful and smiling—flourishes.[50]

In the same way, every poem makes language true and real, because language is intrinsically poetic:

> And new and foreign languages are not only those we call such in the usual designation, but—to stick to the reality of the thing and the rigor of the concept—every word we hear is a new and foreign language, because it was never uttered before and is not identified with any of those said before, and we, upon hearing it for the first time, only understand it by one of those acts of consensus and fondness that we have recognized as fundamental and essential. [. . .] And any

form of poetry created and recreated by us in our minds is nothing but an expression of a new language, because the illusion that poets, and people who generally speak, make use of articulate sounds as of tiles that are ready-made and only need to be put in one order or another, is a mythology worthy of lexicographers and grammarians, which I shall not linger here to refute.[51]

On the other hand this is a reaffirmation—with some sort of absolute continuity—of the unique and indivisible character of beauty, which however occurs time after time in the work of art. This contradiction, be it apparent or real, is greatly significant. Following Croce in his considerations, one understands that the uniqueness of beauty is precisely what protects its identity and defends the possibility of its multiple manifestations. In other words: if beauty derives from the unity intrinsic to the motion from intuition to expression, then history and culture are ultimately irrelevant to expression, so that, for example, it does not really matter if a work of art has been conceived in Borneo or in Northern Africa or in fourth-century Athens.

This all relies upon the fact that an artwork mirrors a single spiritual movement, which can also lead to formally different outcomes. With a single gesture, extreme but—as always—not overtly declared as such, Croce banishes the totality of aesthetic categories, as well as literary genres and the meaning of historical and cultural differences; and he does it for the sake of the universality of beauty. He comes awfully close to even overthrowing the boundaries of different arts, and there is actually no reason why this should not happen. Croce tackles again the issue of beauty and its unity and indivisibility:

> Thus, the category of beauty is one and indivisible, although its individual manifestations are endless, and although these can be grouped into classes—not at all empirical, as usual for classes—, and they have nothing in common with the speculative distinctions of the speculative concept. Furthermore, when one examines the various forms that one estimates to be able to speculatively distinguish within beauty (like those that once were called by the aesthetics "modifications of beauty," and it was the "sublime," the "tragic," the "comic," the "humorous," the "graceful," and so on) one does not find anything other than abstractions based on single groups of beautiful works referable to their matter—their matter and not their form, which alone is beauty.[52]

A few pages later, Croce negates the national, local, social character of beauty, and states:

> Therefore, it is all the more worth energetically reaffirming the indivisibility of beauty, the only category of judgment, because the divisions that are now made in it do not just break, as the oldest did, the aesthetic unity of the human race, but destroy humanity itself, closing it in circles foreign to each other, irreconcilable and perpetual enemies.[53]

Once every distinction has been relativised in light of the absolute actuality and cogency of beauty, there is no reason why one should not take the final step: that is, to acknowledge that even the limits, or better yet, the differences among the various arts are a secondary element, inessential when compared to the monocratic centrality of beauty. However, Croce does not want to cross the Rubicon, even though coherence would demand it. If he entirely accepted the consequences of his thinking, he would also have to say that the very means of expression, and not only genres, are basically inessential and secondary in comparison to their artistic outcome. In principle this would represent a sort of authorization of their union, of their blending in a fruitful collaboration. Taking the outcome of this issue, but not its terms, to its extremes, beauty—of which Croce celebrates the great twentieth-century apology—would eventually become something like a gigantic synesthetic construction that lives entirely on its occurring, which however always presents itself as absolute. Art would thus flow back into life.

This is the most strenuous defense of beauty in the whole twentieth century. As we have seen, this is not an extreme, late-classical offshoot in the avant-garde era. It is precisely the opposite, at least potentially: the (implicit) ideal of a total work of art, which lives only as an event, in its proximity to life, and thus unexpectedly relates to Heidegger's essay "The Origin of the Work of Art."

Chapter IV

From Negativity to the Event

Adorno after Heidegger

Philosophy of Art as Rearguard

At this point, a fundamental question arises: does the twentieth century have its own ideal of beauty? Or is this epoch doomed to ugliness? It goes without saying that these issues are so peremptory they border on brutality, so little philosophic in their demanding a yes or a no— answers that are hard to give so drastically. However, the peremptoriness of this question is what allows some progress to be made on this subject.

In any case, I want to tackle this issue head on. The question about the beauty or ugliness of twentieth-century forms of art classified as avant-garde depends on the actuality—or more, the persuasiveness—of the classical structure of the philosophy of art, which first appeared at the end of the eighteenth century and continued to develop in the following years. In short, whether avant-garde art can be considered beautiful is a philosophical question that can be answered competently only by an art that is inspired by philosophy. That is, it depends on philosophy whether art is beautiful or not. This is no norm, but rather a consideration historically grounded on the tenth book of Plato's *Republic*.

Of course this is paradoxical, but whether something can be considered beautiful depends on the usage of the concept. So the crisis of the beautiful is first of all a metaphysical crisis, which depends on the difficulty of unifying all the artistic phenomena within the metaphysical concept of beauty. The latter is an ultimate paradigm of meaning, which went from the heights of metaphysics to the suburbs of the philosophy of art, but still remembers its origin.

Therefore, to deal with the concept of beauty it is necessary to state that it lives only as long as an art inspired by philosophy is possible; when this stops existing, so does the very concept of beauty.

But there's more. Without philosophy there is no art, and this goes even further: without philosophy there is no beauty. After all, art embodies a fallen transcendental that stems from beauty in its original appearance. The comparison between aesthetics and artistic avant-garde reveals precisely a tension of this kind, in which the ideal of beauty—maybe contradicted, distorted, pained—lives on in a relationship of dialectic polarity with an art that, despite all, does not give up on its philosophical inspiration.

In this respect, it is hard not to think of a philosophical witness of an artistic avant-garde such as Theodor Wiesengrund Adorno, who always remained true to the bond between aesthetics and metaphysics in a manner that was as strong as it was actually extreme and almost residual. His is an extreme testimony also as regards the historical awareness of his own position: Adorno still clings to the belief that the truth, or better, the "aesthetic" truth can be proclaimed solely and exclusively by philosophy. This is a conscious practice of the paradox. And in this case the paradox does not merely protect the proximity and the distance between metaphysics and aesthetics by means of a delicate pas de deux. There is more, and all this runs through the whole structure of metaphysics, repeating once again—maybe for the last time—the articulation of medieval transcendentals. *Ens, unum, verum,* and *bonum* all come into play, inseparable from one another. In Adorno's aesthetics, the artwork as *res (ens)* by means of its almost monadical identity (*unum*) justifies the construction of an alternative (*bonum-verum*) to the "totally administrated" society that appears as a "bad totality." Here beauty, the last-born child, lines up next to its elder siblings.

According to Adorno, it is philosophy that makes art the nonconceptual witness of the concept, and that therefore makes it true. In this regard what's fundamental is the system of limits that produces an almost geometric system of distances and proximities, of reciprocal recognitions and hierarchies that make themselves recognizable and moreover exclude undue overlaps.

The link connecting metaphysics and aesthetics on a theoretical level is the clearest thing that can initially be taken from Adorno's system. As his readers well know, this link relies not on the alliance between the two terms, but on their opposition. It is far from being a harmonious bond; nevertheless, as it often happens, the components of this couple cannot be separated from one another. Negativity is constantly present in Adorno's thinking, so that in the end aesthetics proves the coherence of the ontological system, while this system experiences itself in the sui generis concreteness of aesthetics. This is a sort of reversed Platonism: after Auschwitz, beauty cannot dwell in this world, precisely because this world does not welcome the other transcendentals: *unum*, and above all *verum* and *bonum*.

Despite everything, despite the emphasis placed on contradiction, this is about a sort of extreme, modern appearance of a past that does not cease to be relevant to the present: it leans towards the present with its critical and architectural system. In other words, this is the extreme appearance of an ancient architecture that already shows the chinks and cracks to come in its design full of negativity. It is almost an outpost whence to watch the present ripen in its multiple, unseizable, lost, ineffable inclination towards beauty. Moreover, the present can be conceived only in terms of difference and detachment, and therefore by its proximity to aesthetic metaphysics.

In fact, this is the peak of the revival of Platonism in art, or, if you will, of the wholly Platonic character of the philosophy of art. Art and its dubious truth are again, maybe for the last time, conceived *sub specie philosophiae*. The philosophical consideration of art thus almost arrogantly becomes the only way to ascertain its truth. It is as if from the tenth book of *The Republic* to Adorno there had been only this one contradiction, the one that seeks to absorb art and verify its truth in the light of the concept; this is perfectly overthrown by Nietzsche, who instead seeks to include the concept into artistic becoming. Following this path, one arrives to an aesthetics such as Adorno's (which is the ultimate, refined conclusion of this reasoning), according to which philosophy finds once more its (asymmetrical) alter ego in art, while art—maybe for the last time—resolves the problem of its truth.

Thus Adorno concludes the long journey that joined aesthetics and metaphysics through the philosophy of art. To evaluate the meaning of this conclusion is ultimately the meaning of this book. The outcome of this evaluation, moreover, is far from predictable. It would all be too simple to express pleasure for an art that finally has escaped the net of metaphysics, an art that is finally just art and nothing else, escaping its extrinsic and abstruse tie to the concept. And so on. . . . As we shall see, the problem is extremely complex, and the conclusions are hard to draw.

When art becomes completely autonomous, it ends up losing any relationship with rationality, which used to be intrinsic to it and traditionally connected it, through beauty, to the sphere of values and to the other transcendentals, in particular to verum and bonum. By losing the connection to its metaphysical roots, art risks turning to irrationality, a risk that, by the way, is intrinsic to autonomous art. There's more: this inevitably ends up damaging the discursivity and communicability that makes art an essential part of culture. Thus art becomes autonomous to all intents and purposes, or better, it becomes "deprived" in every sense. Indeed, it becomes such because it has been deprived of the greatest part of its communicability, but also because its enjoyment is restricted to connoisseurs and experts and to the market that complies with their esoteric requests. And if this is how it goes, there is not much to be done. It is hard to make clear evaluations to make an axiological assessment of art; instead it is extremely easy to get lost in its inscrutable practices, which belong to the artists-sorcerers and their apprentices.

Adorno: From *Negative Dialectics* to Aesthetic Utopia

But now it is necessary to suspend these considerations and go back to them more in detail later. It is also necessary to deal with Adorno's rather difficult theoretical system, insisting on the bond between ontology and dialectics on which everything else depends. To get straight to the point, Adorno believes that behind the theoretical instance lies the ethical one: dialectics must be thought over to try to use it as an instrument to criticize reality. In Adorno's view, reality represents—from its totalitarianisms to mass culture—what Hegel defined a "bad totality": in other words, a universe that is autonomously organized in terms of appearance, but completely heterodirected in terms of essence, which seems to give freedom to its components, while they are actually forced to bow to its will.

In this respect, it surely becomes essential to address Adorno's *Negative Dialectics* (1966), in which he develops a perspective on dialectics that is both technical-philosophical and of general, methodic, and ontological interest at the same time. These things go together and at the same time reveal one of the central motives of Adorno's philosophical strategy: in his view, it is impossible to disentangle the two perspectives—à la Hegel—when it is precisely their being intertwined that outlines a deeply critical attitude towards Hegelian ontology. In a sense, Hegel's and Adorno's paths run parallel to each other.

The impossibility to separate ontology and dialectics wholly shapes Adorno's and Hegel's approaches, but only in that the one is the exact opposite of the other; and Adorno—who cannot be understood without Hegel—is the programmatic, most complete overthrow of Hegelian ontology. In Adorno, a system of reciprocal intolerance is established between dialectics and ontology; and this intolerance is also a denunciation of reality. To use Adorno's words, "after Auschwitz," philosophy must give up on any temptation to legitimate reality and so must art. This is precisely what avant-garde art must do, at least theoretically. Contrary to Hegel, Adorno thinks that dialectics does not lead to a being that should be its fulfilment; on the other hand, if this fulfilment occurred, it would be a betrayal of ontology itself in its nature of outcome and accomplishment. A false accomplishment, an undue apology of reality would take the place of the legitimate fulfilment, which is not permitted here and now.

It is well known that Adorno wanted to open his *Aesthetic Theory* (which was published posthumously) with a motto, a sentence by Friedrich Schlegel: "One of two things is usually lacking in the so-called Philosophy of Art: either philosophy or art."[1] It is also universally known that Adorno wanted to dedicate his book to Samuel Beckett. This is important evidence, which leads straight to the core of the issue debated above. Adorno is the author who dealt with artistic avant-garde more than any other, and made of this topic the center of his aesthetics. It could be said that, as far as aesthetics is concerned, before being Hegel's disciple, Adorno is Plato's disciple—albeit up in arms against his master. In other words, Adorno's aesthetics is characterized by a hand-to-hand fight between art and philosophy, which is the real antithesis—much stronger that Nietzsche's—to the Platonism of aesthetic theory; besides, this antithesis is totally within the polemical target that is being objected to. Thus the comparison between aesthetics and artistic avant-garde does nothing but shed light on the significance and importance of this unresolved tension. It is the conflict between art and philosophy, in which—to anticipate the issue—art tends to win over philosophy and to appropriate the truth that philosophy would have given art on the basis of its own rational authority. But this can be only a half-victory.

From the comparison between aesthetics and artistic avant-garde emerges precisely a conflict of this nature: art challenges the truth of the concept for both moral and theoretical reasons, but on the other hand it cannot do without it. After all, once again there is no art without philosophy. In Adorno's aesthetics art is in a contradictory and paradoxical relationship with philosophy—a sort of nostalgic aversion. It is an agnition that necessarily fails to happen. What is the term of this philosophical agnition? This is the heart of the problem. It is beauty: it appears here again in its ancient and most eminent form, which delivers it to nature and myth (and therefore to the philosophy that examines them), rather than to art.

So now beauty represents what art can no longer be: its own metaphysical destination, which cannot be reached and can no longer coincide with its mundane destination. Adorno thinks that a just world could maybe do without art, because it would enjoy living beauty. But since this is not the case, beauty becomes independent from the world and—at least in negative terms—regains its old prerogatives and its imperious splendor. Beauty, which is now again a metaphysical ideal in every possible sense, experiences a contradictory time in art: a suffering and lacerated destiny. If it realized itself, it would immediately become *kitsch*, ideology, an integral part of the universe whose intrinsic nontruth it exposes. Of course this also has an axiological meaning: beauty must not take root in the world anymore; it mustn't liven up its existence and make its days brighter. This would mean helping falsehood, projecting upon reality a heavenly landscape to hide and exorcise the obscenity of evil. But this also has a direct, both aesthetic and poetological, significance: it represents the condition to start a dialogue with avant-garde art, which chose ugliness and disharmony.

From a strictly aesthetic perspective, the ban of beauty implies that ugliness is even praised because of its artistic meaning (whereas its legitimation had happened long before, at the dawn of German Romanticism with Friedrich Schlegel's essay-study "On the Study of Greek Poetry"). In any case, the aesthetic and metaphysical aspects are once more indissolubly united. From the question of ugliness it is necessary to go back to the purely philosophical connection of dialectics and ontology as Adorno develops it—along with its aesthetic implications—in *Negative Dialectics*. To go back and forth between the two poles of this dialectical relationship is as essential as its interruptions. In fact, the relationship between dialectics and ontology is also an interrupted one: from this perspective, dialectics does not reach the being that should represent its Hegelian *Vollendung*, its fulfilment. If this happened, for Adorno it would be a simultaneous betrayal of both dialectics and ontology. And this would also imply a double—if not triple—disaster, not only in theoretical terms, but also in ethical and aesthetic ones. Adorno writes about this in *Negative Dialectics*, developing the first and the second aspect:

The contradiction is the non-identical under the aspect of identity; the primacy of the principle of contradiction in dialectics measures what is heterogeneous in unitary thinking. By colliding against its own borders, it reaches beyond itself. Dialectics is the consistent consciousness of non-identity. It is not related in advance to a standpoint. Thought is driven, out of its unavoidable insufficiency, its guilt for what it thinks, towards it.[2]

Going back to the theoretical and aesthetic aspects, the realization of beauty would mean that it assumes ipso facto a positive attitude towards the world as it is, thus legitimizing it. But this is not how things are supposed to go. The outcome of Adorno's aesthetics is thus an interrupted dialectics, whose realization can occur only in an indirect way, one that does not escape contradiction and recognizes that the path to follow does not heal the laceration, but keeps the wound open instead. This reintroduces the theoretical link: an indissoluble solidarity pact does not and should not exist between art and philosophy.

But of course at least a negative relationship between them does exist and is also inevitable. In this context beauty cannot be represented; it is not an object of the life of art, except in that it means the nonrepresentable parameter of being constantly negated by it. So, even though it cannot play a positive role, beauty can play a negative one at the highest level. Two are the possible paths at this point: either to continue on the one that has been followed till now (that of a necessary contradiction in the relationship between art and beauty, ontology and dialectics, which continuously goes back and forth between the two poles of this negative but necessary relationship); or to choose another path, a secondary aspect in Adorno's aesthetics but not in the aesthetics of European philosophy in the second half of the twentieth century. The latter introduces an aestheticization of philosophy, as can be deduced from what Adorno writes in *Negative Dialectics*:

This confirms an experience in philosophy which Schöenberg noted in traditional musical theory: you only really learn from this how a passage begins and ends, but nothing about it itself, its trajectory. Analogous to this, philosophy ought not to reduce itself to categories but in a certain sense should compose itself [*komponieren*: to compose musically]. It must continually renew itself in its course, out of its own power just as much as out of the friction with that which it measures itself by; what it bears within itself is decisive, not the thesis or position; the web, not the inductive or deductive, one-track course of thought. That is why philosophy is essentially not reportable. Otherwise it would be superfluous.[3]

It is important to understand why Adorno does not really take this path that he suggested, even if only for a moment. This statement makes him a sort of clairvoyant. In fact, the decision not to take the path to which he nonetheless hints makes him the last bulwark of the classical form of the philosophy of art, which will collapse after him. And it will collapse because of the aestheticization that appears here for the first time and is then held back. Of course, in this passage Adorno clearly sees one of the most important areas of development of twentieth-century aesthetics after him, which leads to the aestheticization of philosophy itself, whose greatest representatives are Heidegger and the deconstructionists (Derrida and his American disciples).

The aestheticization of thought is here like a siren that must be kept at bay, while what must be followed is the other path, that of the conflict between art and philosophy as a constitutional moment of aesthetics itself. As has already been said, this is the principle on which Adorno's aesthetics is built. It is the last great classical construction of the philosophy of art, whose intimate structure is strained to the point of becoming almost transparent and emerging upon its own body, thus finally becoming totally perspicuous. The path of aestheticization is the alter ego of this ancient path and its beyond.

Going back to structural motives, the conflicting relationship between dialectics and ontology is central to Adorno's philosophy, not only from a perspective of philosophical architecture. In this case, it is precisely the theoretical choice that has a series of consecutive and consequent implications even on the personalities and movements that are given voice by Adorno's aesthetics. The choice of a theoretical disharmony (in fact, a pre-established disharmony) influences the other choices about taste, so that Adorno prefers artistic avant-garde and in particular those personalities, from Schöenberg to Beckett and Paul Celan, who are most characterized by that "passion for disharmony" that pervades his works in general. This is a necessary disharmony on a theoretical level, which causes choices on the level of taste and makes Adorno's aesthetics a typical 'trendy' aesthetics also because of what it excludes—or maybe even the most typical. For example, Adorno significantly relegates futurism and Dada (the avant-garde tendencies that promote the aggressiveness of the *Moderne* and conceive themselves as "consequences" of their time) to the margins of his considerations. On the other hand, they are central to those of his foe-friend Walter Benjamin.

Adorno is very clear about the theoretical and aesthetical choice of disharmony, and in *Negative Dialectics* he points out that the truth of both philosophy and art lies in their banishing pseudomorphosis, fictitious integration, and in their loyalty to nonidentity:

> What art and philosophy have in common is not form or patterning
> procedures, but a mode of conduct which forbids pseudomorphosis.
> Both keep faith with their own content through their opposition; art,
> by making itself obdurate against its meaning; philosophy, by not
> clinging to anything immediate.[4]

This is all essential to Adorno, because it is the basis of the utopian structure of his thinking. Even Adorno's utopia, which acquires the extreme darkness of historical experience, can initially be defined only on the basis of this theoretical link. To rephrase it metaphorically, it is a sort of "hopeless hope." Adorno's aesthetic utopia develops in this almost residual area. It is only because both art and philosophy endlessly and desperately long for their reciprocal acknowledgment, only because they both have this endless wish for an impossible agnition, that it is possible to understand and define the utopian structure of Adorno's thinking, which coincides with its vocation to truth.

This is the common ground of art and philosophy, which both seek a truth that transcends them. Taking Adorno even beyond his teaching, this truth has the name of the most uncertain and debated transcendental—that is, beauty. Precisely because of its great distance from reality, beauty can find a strength that it could not reach within "aesthetic art,"[5] within the modern "autonomy of art." Since beauty, the fulfilment of art, lies beyond art itself, art reaches its extra-artistic roots: the kind of beauty that (if Plato's analysis is right) cannot live again in art, but, much more emphatically, only as a cosmic measure.

After all, why else could beauty be defined as an unfulfilled promise of *Bonheur*,[6] if not because it is something more with respect to art itself? That is, with respect to art as manufacture, in the wider sense that goes from the Greek *techne* to modern times; but also, and above all, with respect to aesthetic art. In fact, the latter is the supreme form of anaestheticization of the modern subject, according to the motive of the exoneration from reality proposed by Odo Maquard (which is an extremely frequent refrain in modern aesthetics, starting from the prologue of Goethe's *Faust*).

In short, art is a game for the modern subject, a *dimanche de la vie*, a divertissement. This is important, but also well-known and almost banal. If Maquard was right, it must be added that anaesthetization does not concern only the user, but also the wider sphere of the image, whose influence is modernly restricted to art and, more in general, to the universe of fiction. This theme is dealt with again in the conclusion of this book. At this point, it is enough to observe that art as autonomous art cannot really be a promise of happiness if it is limited to the area of aestheticization: it must go beyond it, regaining the power of beauty—enclosed in the image of Aphrodite escaping chaos by rising from the water, thus giving rise to form—that also intuitively makes beauty akin to truth and good, a sweet promise of integrity and salvation. Adorno leads his readers very close to all this. By means of a really complicated passage that produces a return of thought to itself in order to go beyond itself again, he outlines in *Negative Dialectics* the nontheoretical task of dialectics: "The utopia of cognition would be to open up the nonconceptual with concepts, without making it the same as them."[7]

A few pages later, he makes his stance even clearer:

> The concept cannot otherwise represent the thing which it repressed, namely mimesis, than by appropriating something of this latter in its own mode of conduct, without losing itself to it. To this extent the aesthetic moment is, albeit for totally different reasons than in Schelling, not accidental to philosophy. [. . .] The philosophical concept does not dispense with the longing which animates art as something non-conceptual. [The concept, the organon of thought] and nevertheless the wall [*Mauer*: external wall] between this and what is to be thought through, negates that longing. Philosophy can neither circumvent such negation nor submit itself to it. What is incumbent on it, is the effort to go beyond the concept, by means of the concept.[8]

It is precisely here that the concept finds its freedom, a freedom that ultimately coincides with an aesthetic movement, with the freedom given to the other, understood as a sort of donation of being that frees the other, thus establishing and creating it at the same time. It is some sort of true aesthetic freedom that relies on a contradictory movement: the one that gives the other its own irreducible identity.

This passage opens up the last chapter of the historical path of philosophy of art, in which the philosophical truth attests the very existence of art. This happens by means of the extreme, almost aphasic distance that comes in between the two levels. "Nach Auschwitz." "After Auschwitz," Adorno says repeatedly, nothing can be the way it used to be, free from the contamination of horror. The duty to remember, however, is not merely a warning to remember for those to come. Quite importantly, it also has implications on the epistemic structures of aesthetics, an unanswerable and in many ways disturbing meaning: the distance between philosophy and art has become so great that their ancient bond is close to dissolution.

A Hopeless Hope

At this point it is legitimate to talk about a sort of hopelessness of the philosophy of art, which with Adorno has reached its last phase, in which its truth is exposed and the founding tension between art and philosophy is taken to extremes. This is a sort of double hopelessness: on the one hand, it is the hopelessness of philosophy of art that reaches its end. On the other hand, it is precisely this structure that, when its laceration becomes irreconcilable, shows a sort of hopeless tension—almost, so to speak, one last struggle. This is in contrast with beauty, which bears integrity and harmony. As is known, Adorno believed that this produces a negative aesthetical ideal: the "black ideal." How should one interpret the metaphor of darkness evoked by this ideal? Is it to be interpreted as a metaphor only of darkness connected to sadness, or even to a radical feeling such as hopelessness? Or could it also have a somewhat positive connotation?

Although it might seem incoherent with the most immediate reading of Adorno's text, I wish to choose the second option. It is no unjustified path: from a purely conceptual perspective, it is the most logical and rigorous one. Basically this means that on this path—though in a negative way—art encounters its metaphysical origins, that is, beauty. After Auschwitz art cannot, or better still must not be beautiful. This is maybe the most radical negation of beauty in art ever. The underlying Platonism of the modern and contemporary aesthetic theory thus emerges overwhelmingly. It even overcomes Plato's condemnation of art in the tenth book of *The Republic*, which did not really condemn the fact that art should be defined as beautiful, but rather posited that the quality of this beauty be restricted to appearance and never reach a further and more authentic destination. In light of the dramatic historical circumstances of its time, Adorno affirms something more serious and deep; it has nothing to do with the legitimation of ugliness in art, which has a much more ancient origin in Friedrich Schlegel's text *On the Study of Greek Poetry* and then in Karl Rosenkranz's *Aesthetics of Ugliness*.[9] In Adorno's view, art must not be beautiful. It is an explicit pronouncement in favor of ugliness:

Art must take up the cause of what is proscribed as ugly, though no longer in order to integrate or mitigate it or to reconcile it with its own existence through humor that is more offensive than anything repulsive. Rather, in the ugly, art must denounce the world that creates and reproduces the ugly in its own image, even if in this too the possibility persists that sympathy with the degraded will reverse into concurrence with degradation. [10]

This does not mean that beauty loses any meaning whatsoever or that it is no longer an ideal orientation. In this context, art meets beauty as something that transcends it and does not belong to it, while in ugliness it sees the exemplum of its necessarily unreconciled nature. To break the ban of beauty would be fatal for art; on the other hand, it is precisely the compulsoriness of this ban that makes art sad:

The affinity of all beauty with death has its nexus in the idea of pure form that art imposes on the diversity of the living and that is extinguished in it. In serene beauty its recalcitrant other would be completely pacified, and such aesthetic reconciliation is fatal for the extra-aesthetic. That is the melancholy of art. It achieves an unreal reconciliation at the price of real reconciliation. [11]

This provides works of art with a somehow unstable status: they are oriented towards what lies beyond them. They are forms in search of being. They seek their truth elsewhere— that is, in beauty, which has escaped art and has withdrawn into the mysteries of metaphysics. The philosophical agnition thus occurs through absent beauty, and this causes the artworks to always be looking towards the sky, ideal and offended, from their earthly collocation. Adorno writes about this in *Aesthetic Theory*, mainly in relation to the beauty of nature:

Nature is beautiful in that it appears to say more than it is. To wrest this more from that more's contingency, to gain control of its semblance, to determine it as semblance as well as to negate it as unreal: This is the idea of art. This artifactual more does not in itself guarantee the metaphysical substance of art. That substance could be totally null, and still the artworks could posit a more as what appears. Artworks become artworks in the production of this more; they produce their own transcendence, rather than being its arena, and thereby they once again become separated from transcendence. The actual arena of transcendence in artworks is the nexus of their elements. By straining toward, as well as adapting to, this nexus, they go beyond the appearance that they are, though this transcendence may be unreal. Only in the achievement of this transcendence, not foremost and indeed probably never through meanings, are artworks spiritual. Their transcendence is their eloquence, their script, but it is a script without meaning or, more precisely, a script with broken or veiled meaning.[12]

This "something more" is precisely the hopeless hope I have mentioned above. Herein lies the beauty-less destiny of contemporary artworks, which look to beauty philosophically, as if it were something that does not belong to them artistically. This is the paradox of Adorno's aesthetics, which I have tried to reconstruct in its various theoretical steps to reach its purely aesthetical developments. It is the paradox according to which there is an unbridgeable gap between ontology and dialectics, and the same goes for artwork and beauty. Rightfully and permanently, dialectics is no longer allowed into ontology, just like the artwork is no longer allowed into beauty: however, this tie is necessary and inevitable. Or at least it is such within that noble (if not ancient) philosophical tradition whose remotest forefather is Plato, but which was historically developed by German Romanticism, then by Hegel, and finally by Adorno. Any alternative path would lead to the end of aesthetics as a philosophy of art: it would dissolve both if the univocal relationship between art and philosophy failed (this happens, for example, in Martin Heidegger), and if (but this is less probable) beauty triumphed over the evils of the world and silenced the efforts of the concept once and for all—which is what Adorno despaired for.

In his view, the last ideal residue, which protects the transcendence of beauty, is the black ideal: "To survive reality at its most extreme and grim, artworks that do not want to sell themselves as consolation must equate themselves with that reality. Radical art today is synonymous with dark art; its primary color is black."[13]

From Adorno to Benjamin, from Jünger to Heidegger

Is it possible to go beyond that metaphorical goal represented by Adorno's aesthetics? Can one take a step beyond the "leonine clause" between art and philosophy proclaimed since the origins? Is there something beyond? Before answering these questions, it can be said that this "beyond" has at least a name, which does not sound new: "aesthetic nominalism." In other words, now there is no certain definition of art that includes all the objects that pertain to it. When such a definition is missing, anarchy and conventionalism are a real danger: it is enough to agree upon it, and then anything can be defined art from a certain point of view, according to the position it takes (as an object in an art gallery or in a museum, for example). This is the real, most authentic philosophical (but not only philosophical) danger that arises now and leaves Adorno's negativity behind. Once philosophical truth has ceased to exist, where can one find the scattered limbs of that corpse called "art"?

From the viewpoint of the history of aesthetics, it seems only logical to formulate a totally counterfactual hypothesis, which thus becomes ipso facto theoretical. It can be summarized in the following question: is it possible to analyze Heidegger and Benjamin not only contra, but also after Adorno? (This "after" is totally theoretical and is mainly developed by contemporary thinkers.)[14] So this is the central question here. If in Adorno's exercise of negative criticism one can find the ultimate and key moment of the relationship between art and philosophy, which produced the downfall of the philosophy of art, Benjamin's and Heidegger's "aesthetic nominalism" does not represent a successive step, but actually—to use Heidegger's words—"another beginning".

If that's the case, at least from this point of view, it is not that Adorno comes after Heidegger (considering the purely aesthetic texts), or that he stands far from him (to stick to the dates of birth and death); rather, he comes *before* Heidegger. But before talking about Heidegger, it is necessary to at least touch upon a thinker who is objectively much closer to him, in spite of the theoretical distance between them: Walter Benjamin. In fact, Adorno has to fight nominalism both at home, when he has to deal with Benjamin and the idea of the end of the aura, and at a long distance, in his debate with Heidegger.

The essays that mark this turning point are strangely coeval: they were written between 1935 and 1936. The places in which they were conceived and drafted signal the great distance between the two thinkers: Paris for Benjamin's essay "Art in the Age of Mechanical Reproduction," and Freiburg im Breisgau for Heidegger's conference "The Origin of the Work of Art." They both suspend the relationship of reciprocal acknowledgement between art and philosophy, accepting and almost appropriating the process that Adorno called "deartification of art," in which the aesthetic difference occurs and art gets closer to reality.

From now on, art will not aim at ideals, but at being reality as it happens, thus becoming itself an event. This is the point where Benjamin and Heidegger are the closest to each other, starting from which their two perspectives take deeply different paths. Benjamin is led by a sympathy for Dada and a theoretical inclination towards the new art of filmmaking. He looks to an art that is becoming a "thing" (think of Dada) and getting closer to the structure of Marx's exchangeable good. On the other hand, Heidegger sees the origin of the work of art as an event in poetry, as a sort of original myth.

To get to the core of this issue, it is well known that Adorno sees in Benjamin a sort of deviation: the loss of every critical potential of the work of art. In Benjamin's view, the work of art has become a pure event and thus has no longer any inclination towards transcendence. It has come close to the commercial good precisely by losing its aura, that ineffable something that suspends its status and makes it different from the world. Benjamin positively affirms that, with the fall of the aura, "the work of art becomes a creation with entirely new functions, among which the one we are conscious of, the artistic function, later may be recognized as incidental."[15]

The fall of the aura hampers the transcendence of the artwork and produces what Adorno calls "deartification of art." Now the artwork can be infinitely reproduced for a public of anonymous clients. This is how the aesthetic universe without aura—as it appears not only in the great essay "Art in the Age of Mechanical Reproduction," but also in "Paris, Capital of the Nineteenth Century"—declares the complete transformation of use value into exchange value, which Adorno condemned in a Marxian manner. The reified universe without transcendence, in which art and commodity are ambiguously interchangeable, is characterized by a perverted and yet fascinating development. In Benjamin's view, the Parisian *Passages* are the extreme triumph of the commercial good; however, this is not only a Marxian fetish, but also a phantasmagorical, dreamlike image (*Traumbild*), which from this perspective is closely related to aesthetic appearance and maybe also to beauty. Thus, the commodity embodies the ambiguity of dialectics—a dialectics that is immobilized in its object.[16]

This is when the phantasmagorical character of the commodity turns into a utopia, anticipating a further, critical step in Benjamin's aesthetic considerations: his stance in favor of the technical reproducibility of the work of art, its loss of aura and its bending to serialization. The end of beauty appears here in the downfall of the contemplative, ecstatic character of the aesthetic experience, which is substituted by its shocking nature. The cult value of the artwork related to its hic et nunc, which is connected to the aura, is more and more often substituted by the expositive one. According to Benjamin, this is the basis upon which the qualitative transformation of the work of art establishes itself. What happens with avant-gardes and Dadaism is here paradigmatic, in that it takes moral indignation as its usual practice, to an even greater extent than scandal. The expositive value is here provocatively emphasized, to the point that everyday objects are polemically imposed as artwork on a disconcerted public.

But Benjamin wants to go even further: he wants to overcome what he calls the "packaging" typical of a strictly moral dimension in order to free the potential of art as closer to life. In this context, the paradigmatic form of art is filmmaking, as it has finally reached the masses (which instead arouse Adorno's suspicion, because they derive from a domination that does not allow individuals to be such). Since artworks get closer to their consumers, even the status of the aesthetic experience changes, going from ecstatic to "distracted." The disaggregation of the very status of the artwork leads to the fact that there is no object *strictu sensu* to turn to; it is rather something one has to get closer to; "the distracted mass absorbs the work of art," Benjamin says, thus dissolving the fixity of its whole,[17] making it more and more akin to an event: a historical one, which is not atemporal as beauty is or claims to be. And it is the event-like character of the artwork and of the aesthetic experience that leads from Benjamin to Heidegger. Here it must be remembered that Benjamin's shock, caused by the aesthetic experience, and Heidegger's *Stoß*, the impact one perceives when encountering a work of art, are quite similar in that they both refer to an initially blind experience of the artwork, or at least one that initially lacks a philosophical *lumen*.[18]

Martin Heidegger's consideration thus becomes crucial in this context for a variety of interconnected reasons that, in comparison to Benjamin, amplify and specify the event-like character of the artwork mentioned above. It is precisely this character, philosophically developed by Heidegger, that will definitely destroy the foundations of the philosophy of art. This is important also because it shows—even from a historiographical point of view—that Heidegger's turning to the original connection of myth, poetry, and event (toward which Adorno declares all his hostility),[19] is far from configuring a regressive position within contemporary aesthetics; rather, it reveals all its relevance to the present. Paradoxically, the enhancement of the event-like character of the artwork will also lead to the final disappearance of beauty. At the same time, the double-bind relationship between art and philosophy will fade, causing the downfall of the aesthetic continent itself.

To make a more detailed consideration after all these anticipations, I wish to dwell on something absolutely crucial. That is, one must never forget that Heidegger has explored an insidious territory, which Adorno almost avoided to enter: nihilism. Passing through these areas that were almost completely unknown to Adorno,[20] Heidegger built his own space within negativity and beyond, and also beyond the structure oriented towards Hegelian negativity. This is the basis upon which he was able to turn to a hermeneutics of the work of art. In this light, the nature of the work of art takes on the nature of an event. To do this, Heidegger had to go through someone that, in his interpretation, had become much more than a single thinker, but a whole continent of thought: Friedrich Nietzsche.

In Heidegger's view, Nietzsche represents the fulfilment of a journey that ends the history of metaphysics. From this perspective, Nietzsche is the peak of Western metaphysics, which as a whole seeks to resolve all the previous forms by reducing them to one: the will to power understood as "will to will." Nietzsche's teachings are, for Heidegger, extremely relevant because they reveal the destiny of metaphysics as a prevarication of beings (*Seiendes*) on being (*Sein*), even if they are not as effective on the present as his Nazi interpreters, especially Alfred Bäumler, claimed.[21] The whole of Heidegger's interpretation aims at showing that Nietzsche fulfils the history of metaphysics understood as a progressive oblivion of being, until its complete disappearance. On this path, one can find that sort of formal 'disaster' observed in the previous chapters; it appears as some kind of omnipresent, exasperated activity of the will to power, which is extremely harmful to the distinction of form that beauty requires. In this context, it may be useful to remember that in Heidegger the will to power loses any anthropological significance, any specific roots, and develops as the place where metaphysics ends.

On the other hand, one must also bear in mind that, of Heidegger's lectures on Nietzsche, the opening one focuses precisely on "the will to power as art." What Nietzsche and then Heidegger find interesting about art is its energetic aspect, its ability to sense the becoming, to encapsulate it in a form that is never definite, but always has to open up again and delve back into the world from which its journey started. In short, one could say that both Nietzsche and Heidegger have no particular interest in what Odo Maquard called "aesthetic art." On the contrary, they are both inclined to consider aesthetic art on the basis of a determination that precedes it and invents it. This is the conceptual gesture that stops the becoming, reducing it to being and bringing it back to it. As Heidegger states in "European Nihilism":

When Nietzsche himself insists that being, as "life," is in essence "becoming," he does not intend the roughly defined concept of "becoming" to mean either an endless, continual progression to some unknown goal, nor is he thinking about the confused turmoil and tumult of unrestrained drives. The vague and hackneyed term "becoming" signifies the overpowering of power, as the essence of power, which powerfully and continually returns to itself in its own way.[22]

Regardless of what is being here outlined in relation to the interpretation of Nietzsche—that is, the connection between will to power and eternal return—it must be said that what Heidegger's Nietzsche is particularly interested in is form when it is still structuring itself, rather than form in its ultimate and definite configuration. This implies that Nietzsche, according to what Heidegger himself declares, conceives form from the perspective of its particular *Wirklichkeit*: its particular active reality and effectiveness. This nondescriptive conception of form, which aims at the latter's plastic configuration, induces Heidegger to oddly move away from aesthetic art, which he observes, so to speak, in a genetic phase, long before the aesthetic one (that is, the phase in which art enters museums). Precisely because form is seen first of all from the point of view of its becoming, in a plastic, "soft" phase, it cannot oppose nihilism.

In this case, this is testified not by the direct comparison with Adorno, but by the more indirect and complicated one with Ernst Jünger. The juxtaposition of two figures so different from each other such as Adorno and Jünger may seem odd; however, they both seem—in different periods—to rely on the idea that form can be an opposing element: the first thinks that form opposes the totally administered world, whereas the latter thinks it opposes nihilism (which is very closely related to the totally administered world). Heidegger comes back to this several times, addressing Jünger in the famous essay "Concerning 'The Line.'" He distances himself from Jünger in many senses, accusing him of understanding the concept of will to power merely on a descriptive level. In a short text in which he focuses on evaluating what Jünger did and did not understand, Heidegger also states that Jünger grasped that "today's reality is the will to power,"[23] but he failed to see that the will to power is "what is real in reality."[24]

This means that Jünger looked only at the disaggregation without understanding its roots, without seeing the will to power as the dominion of the elementary, its reactivity towards all the forces that nihilistically can no longer unite in a definite form. Heidegger adds that Jünger stops at the description of reality, but does not inquire further into its origin—and this is the crucial point. This is where the path towards the event starts. For Heidegger, when responding to Jünger, there are no free zones that have been protected from nihilism. According to Jünger, the area that nihilism cannot conquer, the virgin land that can remain such, is made of two crucial moments of life: death and love, and the ultimate sphere whence the inner being emerges, expresses itself, and, so to speak, crystallizes—namely, art.

In the essay "Over the Line," listing the zones that resist nihilism, Jünger states:

> It is the gardens to which the Leviathan has no access, around which it hovers angrily. It is mainly death. Like never before, those who do not fear death are infinitely superior even to the strongest temporal power. For this, fear must be propagated continuously. [. . .] The second fundamental power is *eros*; when two people love each other they take ground away from the Leviathan, they create spaces that it does not control.[25]

A few pages later, Jünger adds art and thought to death and love:

> In the domains of Leviathan bad taste reigns, and one also has to count the artist among the most dangerous opponents. The persecution bans the artist. Tyrants, on the other hand, enhance the slaveholders of the spirit. They disgrace poetry. [. . .] It is indeed true that in language the sun still rises.
>
> If in the act of poetizing language curves into spiritual spheres like fertile ground, in thought it roots into the undifferentiated.[26]

Heidegger rejects Jünger's faith in the idea and in a metaphor that leads beyond nihilism. According to Heidegger, the very metaphor of the beyond comes from a conceptual system that is not fit to produce an adequate understanding of nihilism. In this regard, he says:

> So what about crossing the line? Does it lead out of the area of accomplished nihilism? The attempt to cross the line remains at the mercy of a representation that belongs to the realm in which dominates the oblivion of being. And that's why it still expresses itself by the

> fundamental concepts of metaphysics (form, value, transcendence).
> Can the image of the line adequately represent the area of accom-
> plished nihilism? And is the image of the area better?[27]

Heidegger believes that the essence of nihilism is instead to be conceived within the sphere of the oblivion of being, and the same goes for art.

Art autonomously reactivates its relationship with being, without the need for philosophical mediations. According to Heidegger, the work of art destroys once and for all the relationship between art and philosophy that grounded the philosophy of art as represented, perhaps for the last time, by Adorno's aesthetics. Furthermore, to continue with the long-distance comparison with Adorno, the idea of the eventhood of being—or better, the idea that through the artwork it is possible to reach an occurrence of the truth—destroys the idea that form is the antithesis of a content that comes from the outside. Thanks to this step, Heidegger paradoxically finds himself actually *over the line*, beyond the conflicting alliance between art and philosophy of which Adorno, precisely through the idea of form, had been one of the greatest champions and representatives.

The *concordia discors* between art and philosophy is no longer questioned, and therefore even the peculiar association that had established the historical and theoretical continent during Romanticism, and that defines aesthetics as a philosophy of art, fades. If—as Heidegger teaches in his essay "The Origin of the Work of Art"—the work of art embodies and expresses its own truth, if it is the very implementation of the truth, then we find ourselves beyond the continent of aesthetic categories. In fact, this continent is organized within the limits and thanks to the parameters imposed by the jurisdiction of the philosophy of art, whose key issue is the conflict between appearance and truth. Thus art assumes a sort of inaugural character, one that leads to a new, variegated continent whose fundamental principles no longer coincide with that system of correspondences in which beauty was the queen of appearance.

This does not mean that Heidegger stops writing about beauty: as is well known, he does write about it—in somehow antiquated and harmonistic terms—in his essay "The Origin of the Work of Art." This is not surprising, because what he is the least interested in here is precisely the traditional aesthetic-artistic implications of his aesthetic theses. Moreover, the dialectics that supported nineteenth-century philosophy of art (and also Adorno's aesthetics) has completely exploded here. The hostile alliance of art and philosophy, on which Adorno's negativity is based, is now substituted by a relationship that radically transforms the ontology of the work of art, connecting it to the relationship between origin and event. This is what Heidegger declares in the very opening of "The Origin of the Work of Art": "Origin means here that from where and through which a thing is what it is and how it is. That which something is, as it is, we call its nature [*Wesen*]. The origin of something is the source of its nature."[28]

This premise grounds a dialectics that no longer concerns negativity, but—as I indicated above—the event. Heidegger thinks that truth is established in the work of art; and this derives from a dialectics of revelation and concealment thanks to which the work of art is produced as an event. The work of art is carried out by truth, because it stems from this dialectics of revelation and concealment, which is, so to speak, doubled by the conflict between world and Earth, between the universe of already organized meanings and the chaotic background that can renew them. Thus, almost unconsciously, Heidegger determinedly heads towards aesthetic nominalism, and he finds himself in the really variegated (but also aristocratic) sphere of twentieth-century aesthetics: here he is surprisingly close to thinkers such as Walter Benjamin and Benedetto Croce, who are very different from him.

But is it really possible to talk about aesthetic nominalism in relation to Heidegger? Would Heidegger, who praises poetry as the origin of the work of art almost as a myth, adopt an attitude that at first sight is basically minimalistic? In fact, the work of art as event of the truth tends to embody *all* art, all its resources: indeed, poetry. Since the work of art puts into practice the truth in its historicization, it includes all forms of art in a magniloquent gesture. This way it produces an event that is always unique, in principle totalizing and therefore substantially incomparable to any other. This is a new totality, whose interpretation is no longer supported by the historical conscience that had ignited the long journey of the philosophy of art. The inaugural character of the work of art erases the hermeneutic significance of the historical distance of all the aesthetic categories based on the work of art itself.

Now the work of art is to be interpreted only through itself, through the set of meanings it expresses in a completely original way, according to what, for Heidegger, is shown by Van Gogh's famous *Peasant Shoes*. In other words, the work of art is its own interpretation, which no longer needs that immense deposit of sense that had been sedimenting in aesthetic categories over the centuries. It is no longer philosophy that ascertains the truth of art, but it is art itself that now becomes an occurrence of truth, and therefore an event that is always unique and autonomous, with total control over its meaning. Heidegger writes:

> Poetry is here thought in such a broad sense, and at the same time in such an intimate and essential unity with language and the word, that it must remain open whether art, in all its modes from architecture to poesy, exhausts the nature of poetry. [. . .] The essence of art is poetry. The essence of poetry, however, is the founding [*Stiftung*] of truth. "Founding" is understood, here, in a threefold sense: as bestowing, as grounding, and as beginning. But it only becomes actual in preserving. Thus to each mode of founding there corresponds a mode of preserving. All we can do at present is to make this essential structure visible in a few strokes, and even that only to the extent that the earlier characterization of the essential nature of the work provides an initial clue.

The setting-into-work of truth thrusts up the extra-ordinary [*Ungebeure*] while thrusting down the ordinary, and what one takes to be such. The truth that opens itself in the work can never be verified or derived from what went before. In its exclusive reality, what went before is refuted by the work. What art founds, therefore, can never be compensated and made good in terms of what is present and available for use. The founding is an overflowing, a bestowal. [. . .] Art allows truth to arise [*entspringen*]. Art arises as the founding preservation of the truth of beings in the work. To allow something to arise, to bring something into being from out of the essential source in the founding leap [sprung] is what is meant by the word "origin" [*Ursprung*].[29]

This causes a sort of short circuit between the artwork and art, which endangers all the categories, all the principles of aesthetic comprehensibility, and induces the consumer to sink into its object, which becomes a gift and a hermeneutic event. This is the turning point that was so long wished for. Art is finally free from the domination of philosophy and conquers its emancipation. But its coming of age is much more confused than its adolescent conflicts with philosophy. Now the work of art is certainly free from the control of the philosophical rationality that wanted to subdue it, but it has also lost any transcendental criterion to evaluate itself. It has to understand and propose itself on its own, not without producing a remarkable disorientation in itself and in its users—a disorientation that is still felt today.

Chapter V

The Dissolution of the Artwork
and the Rebirth of Ancient Beauty

Aesthetics as Energetics

The necessity to go through Heidegger and Adorno has led us to the far ends of aesthetics, understood as philosophy of art in its nineteenth/twentieth century characterization, which can be traced back to Romanticism and Hegel. The historical setting of the discourse is methodologically important: it is what organizes all the stages of this book in the conceptual hunt for beauty. In this case, however, the historical setting is perhaps too reassuring. We have reached the edge of the abyss, and it gives us confidence, making us think that there is shelter beyond the darkness and that the future isn't all that scary. But, at least in this case, reality—let's be honest—is far more disturbing than any comforting historical distinction. We have actually reached a limit that puts an end to an era and to the historical journey of a philosophical discipline, at least in its most recent configuration. Gone are the days when it was philosophy that certified the truth of art in the name of the metaphysical ideal of beauty. Once these boundaries are crossed, the artwork finds the extreme solitude of its finally conquered freedom. It is now pervaded by a strange ambivalent thrill of heights.

All of this produces a feeling of powerfulness and powerlessness at the same time. Of course the power of absolute art is unleashed, but this absoluteness is poor, marked by the sense of mourning implicit in its very etymological origin: ab-solutus, free from, detached from. . . . So yes, there is the power of art as self-understanding, rejecting the aid of philosophy. But the realm of its sovereignty is narrow indeed. It is the icy lady of a solitary domain marked by impassable boundaries: it is the rising art system that is establishing itself as a sort of closed circuit from the authors to their audience through the institutions that act as mediums: museums, critics, the market. The art system thus organizes its borders, which are also those of autonomous art. Within these new symbolic and real structures, and with an almost neurotic attitude, art tends to cancel the gesture of detachment that generated it. It seeks to reset the past, to find itself again in its triumphant original fullness, but instead produces the opposite: subsequent destructuring. After all, as to its origins and its ultimate fate—as the reader probably recalls—beauty belongs more to the world than to art.

This is the way—as we have seen—any new form of avant-garde stands as a gesture of protest against autonomous art, arising from the need to find, besides the institutions of art, life. Doing so, avant-garde gives way to deception: it does not go back to beauty (and thus, implicitly, to myth and metaphysics) in order to break away from it again, as it thinks it is doing, but replaces itself with its objective. In this way, coming back to itself, mistaking itself for its own ghost and dramatically freeing itself from it, it tragically dismembers itself: it resolves in its components to meet new syntheses that claim to enshrine the return to its former status, restoring the life from which it was exiled. And yet, each of these components, one after the other, is captured and returned to the art system. And so on.

This is in many ways the exemplary fate of the avant-garde, which combines the power of the absolute art (of Romantic origin) and the destructuring of symbolic codes, along with the need to join art and life again. In this context, surrealism is paradigmatic. In it, the articulated system of the form in its traditional distinctions—form/content, internal/external—undergoes a sort of meltdown, one that sets free the energies structuring the artwork. The latter then orients itself towards new symbolic codifications, resorting to the secret energies arising from the disintegration of the classic structure (just think, for example, of the importance of the unconscious in surrealist poetry). Through this complex and sophisticated work surrealism does not want to stick to the boundaries of art; instead it wants to demonstrate its effectiveness on the world, promoting a political revolution.

From Philosophy to Surrealism

In order to proceed we must now go into the philosophy of surrealism—an oxymoron that is, however, authoritatively supported by thinkers such as Ferdinand Alquié and, perhaps above all, by Georges Bataille. Let us ask the question right now: what happened to beauty in this context? Surrealism indeed proposes its own ideal of beauty and, at the same time, supports the idea—to confirm what I indicated above—that artistic activity should affect life, so as to transform it.

One wonders what beauty goes through in this frame, and how it is even still licit to speak about beauty here. The issue is particularly relevant because surrealism is the movement that radically puts into question the symbolic language of the artwork. It is well known that the surrealist form sinks into the deep layers that disrupt formal structures, both objective and symbolic, moving in the direction of a higher synthesis. Thus, surrealism sets itself along the line of aesthetic modernity, modeling the artistic ideal through its very negation and leading—as we have seen—from Romanticism to twentieth-century avant-garde.[1] The hyperbolic nature of aesthetic modernity appears here in its wide scope: art assumes the seemingly most artificial and least beauty-oriented attitude in order to reopen—in this paradoxical and almost forced way—the path that leads from beauty to life.

Surrealist beauty is not anti-Platonic: it is the kind of beauty that Freud found at the bottom of Platonic *eros*. This does not go against the ancient ideal of beauty: quite the opposite. As noted by Ferdinand Alquié, the main philosopher of surrealism, the protest against beauty made by Breton and friends is conducted in the name of this same ideal. He states: "Breton therefore is not indignant against what is usually called beauty, truth and good if not in the name of a beauty, truth and good that he considers more authentic."[2] Therefore, Alquié goes on, this ideal of beauty is neither commensurable nor objectifiable, conveyed by Platonic eros and making also use of Freud's lesson.[3] Thus the ancient gets closer to the modern. The surrealist eroticization of beauty—after the long break that Kant imposed on modern beauty, which had to be completely unattractive—also coincides with the need to reactivate the original link between beauty and happiness. Beauty is indeed the announcement of a new time,[4] the anticipation of a joy to experience in the here and now of existence.[5]

However, immediacy is not the hic et nunc: it can happen only at the cost of crossing the onyric lands in which the order of reality is destructured and recomposed into a new (critical and even revolutionary) symbolic order. Hence the centrality of a faculty of manifest Romantic ascendant: imagination.[6] This gives rise to an ideal aimed at paradox, almost monstrous in its rejection of classical tranquillity. It's André Breton's "convulsive beauty": a beauty that, by the virtue of its composure and lack of simplicity becomes something unprecedented and marvelous. That's what Breton programmatically states in the first "Manifesto of Surrealism" (1924): "Let us not mince words: the marvelous is always beautiful, anything marvelous is beautiful, in fact only the marvelous is beautiful."[7]

What creates marvel is the dream-like association, which makes unprecedented connections explicit. Lautréamont leads the way: "Beautiful as the chance meeting on a dissecting-table of a sewing-machine and an umbrella."[8] Beauty is therefore a dip into the deep that reactivates its energy and puts it to good use.[9] Here we come—in terms of artistic practice—to the threshold we glimpsed in the previous chapter. Now the aesthetic object—made possible thanks to the synthesis of the marvelous—has lost its unity; and what surrealism does is precisely to break up the unity of the object. However, it also does something opposite: it derives the elements and structure of its subsequent rebirths from this disaggregation. It is a new artistic grammar—a symbolic one, one that discovers the profound connection of being in the symbol. Being itself is thus condensed in the great crucible of beauty—the nucleus in which lurk the problems and their solutions, extreme landing place where the truth is established, the "ultimate form of hope."[10]

To explore the question we have to look at the thought of Georges Bataille, who is undoubtedly the most conscious philosophical witness of surrealism. A student of Alexandre Kojève, like many other protagonists of the French intellectual scene, Bataille followed with enthusiasm his lectures on the *Phenomenology of Spirit* in the 1930s at the École Pratique des Hautes Etudes, Paris.[11] However, Bataille takes Hegel's negativity to extremes. Fascinated by phenomena such as sacrifice and unnecessary waste, he abandons the hall of mirrors of the dialectic; in other words, he leaves behind the possibility that subjectivity may recognize itself in its objectification. Rather, he chooses a path that takes only the first step of the Hegelian movement: that of the subject who is estranged from itself, losing its structure, unleashing the energies that order it. Thus the dialectic becomes, with Bataille, a kind of "energetics." It is in this context that one should also understand Bataille's theoretical and philosophical proximity to the surrealist movement—for him, surrealism is not a poetic, but *the* poetic *par excellence*, the generator of poetry itself, its essence, even.

For Bataille, the heart of surrealist poetics is the principle of automatic writing, therefore a sort of unconscious *poiesis*. In his mind, this principle is a sort of contradiction in terms: nothing is more paradoxical than a technical action directed at an unconscious goal! But there's more: this poetic breaks down the objects it touches upon only to recompose them after dragging them into the 'surreal,' 'supernatural' waters of poetry. In this respect, one could note the influence of Baudelaire and the Romantic legacy. However, for Bataille the surrealist contradiction is more than that: it signifies the dissolution of the formal system, which implodes and turns into an energy system.[12]

Surrealism looks into the depth of things: as Bataille notices following Breton, it wants to recover our psychic energies.[13] From this point of view, Bataille can say that surrealism goes beyond the order of discourse, that it meets the need to "create an impersonal instance," that "it is [. . .] life itself."[14] Looking into the depth of being, it almost magically clears and restarts the fundamental energies that are found as a result of the disintegration of the ancient formal structures. In this regard, Bataille—quoting and radicalizing Breton—recalls that surrealism is oriented towards the "annihilation of being"[15] so as to rediscover its original features. "Certainly every *thing* slips into crime or death, or the excess of joy that destroys it, as the pieces of coal do in the presence of burning fire."[16]

It is the threshold between the sacred and the primordial mystery; its dramatic nature paradoxically goes along with an auratic climate that reflects "the misery and mutism of birth."[17] Venturing into those magmatic lands, sinking deep under the differences, poetry meets nothingness face-to-face. Bataille said that "poetry is sacred insofar as it is *nothing*. The truth of modern poetry is to have deprived poetry of substance."[18] Nothingness—which dismantles the differences—deprives poetry of substance, and makes of it a kind of immense "totipotent" energy field, almost an analogue of the absolute. It outlines a huge creative labor, punctuated by intervals of fullness and void alternating by systoles and diastoles, whence being emerges as a whole. Here poetry finds once again its original foundation in itself. It renews its ancient power and can claim the supreme throne: that of God.[19]

"The impulse of modern art was this
desire to destroy beauty . . ."

We must now make a decisive leap to the other side of the ocean and dwell on abstract expressionism. There we shall find a sort of impressive acceleration of the artwork's breakdown for reasons that impose themselves with even greater force than in the European past. What instead has the same, unchanged power is the urge to recompose the artwork starting from its *disiecta membra*.

Abstract expressionism harbors a sort of metaphysical instinct of contemporary art. Harold Rosenberg, the great American critic who gave the movement its name, points this out:

> One might say that Rothko and his friends constituted the theological sector of Abstract Expressionism. Together with Still, Newman, Reinhardt, Gottlieb (the names suddenly translate themselves into characters of a miracle play), Rothko sought to arrive at an ultimate sign. To this end, he and the other theologicians conceived painting as a kind of marathon of deletions—one of them got rid of color, another of texture, a third of drawing, and so on.[20]

It is a far more radical work of deconstruction than what was profiled in surrealism. It is almost useless to recall that, even in this case, the unconscious plays a major role in the artistic work both on the author's side and on that of the public. Jackson Pollock, in particular, emphasizes this aspect in his famous interview at the Sag Harbor radio station (summer 1950): "The unconscious is a very important side of modern art and I think the unconscious drives do mean a lot in looking at paintings."[21]

The unconscious is a kind of inner necessity of the artwork in its very making. And here we come to one of the most interesting key points regarding action painting: the work is somehow subordinated to the idea that it should represent. From this point of view the meaning of the technique—think of Pollock's emphasis on dripping—recedes before the idea to which the work is devoted. Pollock's technique is surely calculated and spectacular: the particular way he uses the brush lets paint drip from above and land on the canvas, which is laid on the floor. However, this technique—in which chance and necessity are at one—is actually functional to something that transcends it. Pollock stresses this in the abovementioned interview when, asked about the meaning of technique, he replies that what matters is the result and that "technique is just a means of arriving at a statement."[22]

So, the technical choice itself of big canvas—as I better explain later, with regards to other great exponents of United States avant-garde such as Frank Stella and Mark Rothko—is functional to an art that tends to break through the limits of the work in the direction of its transcendent fulfilment. Pollock, with his technique, explicitly wants to open up the limits of the canvas,[23] realizing its transcendent reference. The realization of the work thus takes on an asymptotic character, in the making. In other words, the work tends to take back into itself its components which have come to free themselves from the painting as a place that synthetized them in itself. This is shown by the works made between 1946 and 1950: conglomerates, realized thanks to the almost automatic confluence on the canvas of letters, numbers, and collages.[24]

Thus, it is a venture into the genesis of the image; one may also define this a reactivation of the subjectivity of the image. Pollock's sensational gesture of painting on the floor should probably also be seen in this light. Moving away from the alternative of subject and object, subject and representation— as demanded by the canvas on the easel—Pollock seems to indicate his desire to animate the subjectivity of the work itself, which takes its own components into itself, disaggregating and recomposing them.

It is one of the most violent and acute criticisms that was ever made against aesthetic consciousness, denouncing the insufficiency of the very deconstruction proposed by European avant-garde and cubism in particular. It is no coincidence—despite the many risks related to enclosing different painters in one set—that someone such as Rothko and his friends would seek an absolute sign, as Rosenberg stated. Rothko's aim is also to "dramatize the crumbling of subject matter";[25] he believes that painting should undergo a purification process so that it doesn't express subjectivity, but its opposite: the non-I.[26]

Thus, Rothko's poetics can be defined as the "poetry and agony of self-displacement":[27] a process of purification taken to extremes, in which the disappearance of subjectivity gives way to "absolute" images, in principle infinitely repeatable and with no need of further intervention on the part of artistic subjectivity.[28] The artwork at the edge of the absolute does not reject the idea of its serial reproducibility. We are dealing here with a nonreferential sign, invoking and holding its autonomy. Although this may seem paradoxical, the (at least ideal) step to Andy Warhol is not so long.

Before addressing these times, I cannot help but notice that this is a crucial point, which leads me to address another of the great protagonists of abstract expressionism—namely, Barnett Newman. What is now in question is the autonomy of the image, which has (provisionally) freed itself from the bonds of aesthetic consciousness (only to be reabsorbed within the sprawling mesh of its visible representative: the museum). Thanks to the deconstruction of the work's links with the idea of objectivity, and thus also the correlative ones that related it to the subject, it has now acquired its own complete autonomy. The image now revives its ancient mythical power and wants to draw in to itself and almost swallow the viewer. This veritable mythical revival of the image thematically and consciously appears in a wonderful essay, "The Sublime Is Now," by an artist-philosopher, reader of Aeschylus and Nietzsche, called Barnett Newman.

It is a strategically perfect essay, in which adequate and reasoned philosophical awareness is combined with poetological knowledge. The essay is, first of all, concerned with the American avant-garde in relation to the European strand. That's the meaning of "the sublime is now": this expression puts into question the Greek-Renaissance tradition, in which European modern art is still stuck, according to Barnett Newman. The aim is to free the absolute in the artworks and realize the transcendence of American avant-garde of which I wrote earlier. Newman proposes this thesis in another essay, "The Ideographic Picture," where he states:

> The basis of an aesthetic act is the pure idea. But the pure idea is, of necessity, an aesthetic act. Here then is the epistemological paradox that is the artist's problem. Not space cutting nor space building, not construction nor fauvist destruction; not the pure line, straight and narrow, nor the tortured line, distorted and humiliating; not the accurate eye, all fingers, nor the wild eye of dream, winking; but the idea-complex that makes contact with mystery—of life, of men, of nature, of the hard, black chaos that is death, or the greyer, softer chaos that is tragedy. For it is only the pure idea that has meaning. Everything else has everything else.[29]

In this context, beauty is a misunderstanding or a misconception, which is rooted in the unfair debt of European culture with the Greeks. Barnett Newman says so clearly, addressing a peremptory indictment to the Greek tradition that founds the European sensibility. The absolute of the form, in this tradition, was mistaken for the absolute *tout court*:

> The invention of beauty by the Greeks, that is, their postulate of beauty as an ideal, has been the bugbear of European art and European aesthetic philosophies. Man's natural desire in the arts to express his relation to the Absolute became identified and confused with the absolutisms of perfect creations—with the fetish of quality—so that the European artist has been continually involved in the moral struggle between notions of beauty and the desire for sublimity.[30]

Newman's polemical considerations are guided by a consequent radicalism: they go towards the origins to locate the denial of the sublime in Plato and Plotinus. In other words, the Greek aesthetics fails to break free from the Platonic vision of beauty and value. This view coincides with an ideal of formal perfection; in this way the motif of chaos, which hints to infinity, is deprived of its authority by the sublime. For Newman, the primacy of formal perfection (which also produces the misunderstanding of the sublime) continues with Kant and Hegel, who kept considering the sublime in relation to beauty. The only exception is Burke, who sharply distinguished between the two. Now, the fact that the sublime was mistaken for perfect form has implied the misconception of its deepest nature, says Newman, which is that of the dissolution of form—as testified by some moments of the history of European art, such as the Gothic or the Baroque styles.

According to Newman, the consequences of this misunderstanding pervade European art, which, in the Renaissance, decided to translate the legend of Christ in the forms of the Greek ideal, while the ecstatic power that had been aroused in the Gothic fell into oblivion. The historical account made by Newman is remarkably consistent and expands from the Renaissance to Michelangelo, who amplifies this Greek need to reach the form—such a need translates into the monumentalization of Christ's human figure under the features of a cathedral. The classical movement of European art is therefore an externalization, overlooking and removing the potentially disruptive, "sublime" plunge inward.

A corrective to this trend comes from painting. Painting—as also evidenced by impressionism—is turned towards concreteness and finally finds the inadequacy of the ideal of beauty, so much so that the impressionists themselves were delighted with "bad brush strokes." Here one can see the first glimpse of the profound vocation of modern art, which is to reopen the boundaries of the form, as Barnett Newman says: "The impulse of modern art was this desire to destroy beauty."[31]

This is the task before which modern European art has given up. It engaged in a metamorphosis of formal values without doing away with its fundamental motif: that is, the emphasis of form in its perfection, where one can see the legacy of beauty. Thus—to move on to the sublime and therefore to the different fate of American avant-garde—the final vocation of modern art is close not only to the deep identity of American art, but also to the most profound meaning of America as an alternative: the formal perfection of European art is replaced by an unstable, dynamic propensity to a figurative ideal, which is paradoxical given its constant condition of disquiet and energy in the making.

What the European avant-garde, from Picasso to Mondrian, failed to do because it was stuck in formal and geometric ideals, became a sort of mission on the other side of the ocean. American art overturns the trend of the process started with Michelangelo; it no longer starts from the image of Christ in order to monumentalize it in a cathedral, but delves into interiority and seeks powerful, revealing images starting from innerness itself:

> We are reasserting man's natural desire for the exalted, for a concern with our relationship to the absolute emotions. We do not need the obsolete props of an outmoded and antiquated legend. We are creating images whose reality is self-evident. [. . .] The image we produce is the self-evident one of revelation, real and concrete, that can be understood by anyone who will look at it without the nostalgic glasses of history.[32]

"High and Low"

Thus the image acquires new unprecedented power, as shown by its ability to emerge from innerness and manifest itself in all its expressive scope: as we have seen, it appears in the—both old and new—guise of the sublime. This framework outlines an art oriented toward transcendence: the sublime then looks back and beyond itself, as it is now a bridge to beauty. Again it denies itself, but this time, it does so after finding itself. Featuring an unstable structure and dynamic, it intends to end its uneasiness thanks to the balance of beauty. Again—as had happened with German expressionism (giving credit to some of its greatest interpreters)—the form leans towards transcendence; it seeks an answer that, at least in the case of Mark Rothko, will lead to a kind of tragic and mysterious melee with the absolute.[33]

The transition to New Dada and, above all, to pop art produces—at least from the standpoint of a philosophical consideration of the artistic phenomenon—a radical change of vision. It is a sort of reversal—a change of course that, however, is not absolute. On the one hand, it has to do with a kind of transition from the top to the bottom, as indicated by the title of this section. It is a new direction: the privilege of the expressive energy of the subject is replaced by the inclination to turn back to the world. (Once again) the features of the world, of this world, are what appears under the guise of art: it is the everyday, the usual landscape of modern life that now establishes itself under the spectrum of art forms. Art even replicates the media.

All of this produces a sort of decline of appearance that blends with the world, which culminates with the recovery of reality in its daily nature, as is exemplified by the New Dada and particularly by Robert Rauschenberg, who takes from Dada—think of Marcel Duchamp—something that was above all a provocation: the ready-made, the exhibition of everyday objects as works of art. New Dada sometimes chooses to place itself on a strange ambiguous ridge, remaining suspended between appearance and reality, and sometimes playing—as with Jasper Johns and his American flags—with this ambiguity, thus manifesting a subtle criticism that lies behind the apparent adhesion to the world in its present features. Robert Rauschenberg—as we see later—takes things even further: art must rejoin life.

Contrary to what occurred with the ironic gesture of protest of the Zurich Dada, in the case of New Dada the distance and the dystonia between art and life weigh on art itself, which has to get closer to the world and the ways of modern life. This means that Rauschenberg is inclined towards the world, taking real samples of everyday objects and inserting them in the fabric of his artworks. From this point of view the work is originated (again) by the decline of aesthetic appearance and its subsequent dismemberment. The dizzying precipice that was opened as early as German expressionism seems to continue here on a parallel path. In expressionism, there was an upwards tension to grasp infinity, which undermined the balance of the artwork and gave way to its potential disaggregation. In Rauschenberg there is no longer a failed sublime attempt, but rather its opposite: the decline of aesthetic appearance, which will take an unexpected triumphant turn in Andy Warhol.

In 1955, when he presented a singular mixture of painting and sculpture with samples from reality entitled *Bed*, which is precisely an unmade bed, Rauschenberg was still somewhat following an ancient path which began with German Romanticism: that of art coming down to the banality of the world, to everydayness, to ugliness (I focus on this at the beginning of this book). This way of proceeding is undoubtedly consistent, but in this case it produces an unforeseen outcome. As we see in the first chapter, Romanticism mainly entailed a rejection of the form that, despite its efforts, couldn't find itself in reality. With Rauschenberg, though, the direction is that of a (provisional) rebalancing of the situation thanks to the fact that reality replaces appearance.

In this sense, *Bed* is indeed exemplary: not only does it speak of everyday life and lets us glimpse into the past, but it shows the temptation to be swallowed by the latter. This way, there is now zero distance between appearance, aesthetic image, and reality.

However, even within this path that ideally goes from Rauschenberg to Jaspers Johns, up to Andy Warhol (of whom I say more later), one cannot help seeing a degree of continuity with some aspects of abstract expressionism, and especially the issue of the image and its status. This statement might seem surprising, when dealing with a sort of overturning of attitudes—from the transcendent realization of art to the latter's renewed propensity to set itself in the world. Well, what is usually noticed in this context is the renewed power of the image, its almost mythical ability to capture the person who contemplates it. The image thus regains its ancient virtues, reiterating that it is primarily the subject, and not the object of representation. It no longer belongs to the aestheticized universe of art, but reiterates the legitimate claim to inhabit this world.

Modern thought tends to do without aesthetic difference to take over the world and its forms, as Heidegger had already noted in his "The Origin of the Work of Art." It's almost as if there were a tacit but truly powerful rebirth of what (in the first chapter of this book) I defined "the ornamental vocation" of art as opposed to the "expressive" vocation of aesthetic modernity. The forms of reality—which, note, is "artificial" in its entirety—are also those of art, while the latter express the order of this world. We started from Goethe, and now we seem to come across an unexpected and estranging Goethean revival after the Romantic phase of modern art. Now the forms of art can once again claim to be the forms of reality: in other words, they can claim to be its accomplishment. This is what was defined as "beauty." It's an unheard of claim, and yet it's authentic, revealing, and substantiating the mythological (more than philosophical) nature of truth and beauty on which I dwell at the beginning of this book. And let's not forget—as seen in the introduction—that in medieval transcendentals, truth and beauty went along with *bonum*, thanks to which the world could be taken to be just *because* beautiful and beautiful *because* just.

Thus we have reached the threshold of the definite disappearance of philosophical aesthetics as philosophy of art: in principle, it identifies and limits its territories on the basis of Plato's distinction between truth and appearance, channeling art into the latter. One has to directly address the question to summarize what happened. If you will, in historical terms, this is one of the most blatant reversals of Baudelaire's aesthetics, which is in many ways an icon of aesthetic modernity. Baudelaire's imperative as it appears in "Le voyage" in *The Flowers of Evil* was "au fond de l'inconnu pour trouver du nouveau": to venture into the most extreme abyss of the unknown—death—to find the new. Well, this project seems programmatically denied by New Dada and even more so by pop art, which take everyday life, in its most ordinary aspects, as the object of artistic representation. The sublime and almost heroic effort of Baudelaire's modernity,[34] which starts from the most ineffable or foulest contents to realize form in sublimity, is here discarded completely. This seems to be the programmatic reversal of what Baudelaire stated in "The Painter of Modern Life": "Modernity is the transient, the fleeting, the contingent; it is one half of art, the other being the—eternal and the immovable."[35]

We are now dealing with a subject that has made peace with reality and wants to find its place in its world and in its symbolic universe without getting lost in sublime efforts to safeguard the purity of the art form. This involves—to continue and conclude the brief comparison with Baudelaire—the wide use of the means of expression that Baudelaire had denounced as illegitimate: photography. The latter often becomes for the artist a constituting element or the basis on which to work. This friendly attitude towards reality, on the other hand, is what marks the distance between Dada and New Dada, as testified by their two different ways to propose the ready-made.[36]

It is almost impossible to escape an overused example here: the very well known urinal proposed by Marcel Duchamp under the title *Fountain*, in an exhibition context and in a different position from that of its normal use—as a work of art. With New Dada the issue is set in different terms: Duchamp, in fact, does not present the item with its name, the one that identifies its daily use. Rather he renames it *Fountain*. With this gesture—despite their identification de facto—the gap between appearance and reality is traced and claimed, with a critical function. In suspending the functionality of the object, Duchamp still announces a critical transcendence of aesthetic appearance in that respect and thus also in relation to the world of which it is part. Starting from New Dada and up to pop art in particular, there is a veritably friendly attitude towards the universe of the house and of commercial goods; this is the world where the symbolic repertoire lies nowadays.

Note the markedly American nature of these artistic movements, which express pride and a subtle irony for the world as it is—at least the world they belong to. This path will culminate in an artist that (metonymically, *pars pro toto*!) symbolizes the final goal of the journey of this book: Andy Warhol. This is the final stage of philosophy of art in the twentieth century as I have defined it. In fact, with Warhol we are no longer dealing with a simple bridge between art and reality, taking samples from one into the other: it is a full integration of the two. In many ways Warhol unexpectedly realizes what Goethe had predicted more than two centuries earlier: the forms of reality are themselves artistic and artistic poiesis is no different from the natural one. Warhol's ambiguity in this respect is total, since his poiesis concerns not the first nature, but what Adorno, in the wake of Hegel, had called the "second nature": the cosmos of technological and cultural forms.

Things start taking this direction with New Dada, with Rauschenberg: here, as we have seen, start a "series of encounters with things."[37] At first there seems to be a path leading from art to reality and, therefore, from beauty (which gives things a form) to dejection in a reality that bears the mark of the ugly. One can go further and recognize—with Rauschenberg—that the very distinction between beauty and ugliness is now overcome.[38] But at this point we cannot stop here. The mechanism is well underway, and it is necessary to take one step further. This happens thanks to Warhol: with him, art in fact definitely escapes the representative logic.

Warhol marks the disappearance of representation. The image is not represented, it doesn't refer to something: it *is*, living an autonomous life. Do not be surprised: it is the restoration of the ancient logic of the mythical image, which appears both on Marilyn's seductive face and on the terrible electric chair—in short, in all the mythological and domestic repertoire contemplated by the idea of "being Americans."

In this context—as Arthur Danto rightly noted—Warhol can very well be taken as a philosopher, both through his pictorial work and through his poetic, as testified by *The Philosophy of Andy Warhol*. With him we witness an explicit and intentional descent from the heavens of appearance to the extreme borders of the land of art. To anticipate things, one could say—with Danto—that Warhol brings to completion the endless journey of aesthetic Platonism as well as (I would add) the more recent one of the philosophy of art (which, still, is rather long: more than one and a half centuries!).[39] The distance between art and truth, philosophically certified, is completely abolished now: this also announces the end of a two-thousand-year-long journey—once again started by the tenth book of Plato's *Republic*—according to which art is destined to the lands of appearance, well outlined by the borderline of the truth (= reality) carefully witnessed by philosophical reflection.

Warhol's is a self-aware and explicit poetic. Also through his portrait galleries, he promotes a veritable modern *epos,* an explicit remythicization of the world producing its new heroes, veritable immutable masks, eternal symbols of late modernity. However, Warhol does not merely present the subjects of modern *epos*, but also—in the framework of a lucid and consistent project—the immense landscape of commercial goods populating the contemporary collective subconscious, as well as the manifest or undisclosed desires of those who share it. This must be the place that we all inhabit, "democratically." This is what is clearly stated in *The Philosophy of Andy Warhol*: "Can you see the Blue Room with Campbell's Soup Cans all over the walls? Because that's what Foreign Heads of State should see, Campbell's Soup Cans and Elizabeth Taylor and Marilyn Monroe. That's America. That's what should be in the White House."[40]

Everything, in Warhol's work, rises from its purely objective or even properly object-like character and takes on a magical, semi-subjective, statute—almost as happens to the objects and furniture that fill the mysterious castle of Disney's *Beauty and the Beast*. The image, in this context, acquires once again a mythical status: it's almost a subject. With its features and movements it once again accompanies daily life. The world that, thanks to Warhol, appears to our eyes is paradoxically devoid of emotion, but filled with great animation. Beauty goes back to referring to people as a custom; it accompanies them step-by-step in everyday life. Thus, beauty is now somehow cold and democratic, universally participable and publicly participated. It has nothing to do with sexual attraction or with health:[41] eroticism and the integrity of the form are both excluded. In short, the classical predicates of beauty are now excluded. Warhol is very clear: "The most plain or unfashionable person in the world can still be beautiful if they're very well-groomed."[42]

Once again beauty is part of "normality": once again it is a natural, usual experience—even though it no longer belongs to a flourishing nature, as it did for the ancients. That nature we have bent to our will and left behind. Nature is such only insofar as we have conquered it and turned it into image, just like the rest of the world we share. But this is the very dimension to which we are naturally addicted, which unifies our imagination, which—to be emphatic—links individuals and makes them a truly universal community in the sign of the commodity and its symbolic value, shared (almost) everywhere:

The most beautiful thing in Tokyo is McDonald's.
The most beautiful thing in Stockholm is McDonald's.
The most beautiful thing in Florence is McDonald's.
Peking and Moscow don't have anything beautiful yet.[43]

Thus we reach the veritable definition of the new universality of beauty: it is founded upon the ability to translate different views into one place, thus exemplifying a new, living image universality. In this context, Peking and Moscow represent residues: they are the—symbolic and real—places still unreached by what would later be called "globalization." Also from this standpoint, America represents beauty: it is able to provide the (formal and stylistic) unifying leitmotif of contemporary complexity, creating the image-like melting pot that constitutes the new canon of beauty—albeit threatened by poverty. "America is really The Beautiful. But it would be more beautiful if everybody had enough money to live."[44]

As one can already deduce from all these observations, we are dealing with a kind of great new mythology, a mythology that—fascinating, but also ironic and distant—runs through the symbolic places of contemporary America. It is a cold and sarcastic mythology, able to make even horror decorative through seriality and a cold, critical distance. Think, for instance, of the series of electric chairs that Warhol observes through the filters of photography and superimposed color: This process makes them similar to grotesque ornamental shapes, now oblivious to the horror they represent.

The same can be said of his portraits, which are a kind of cosmogony of the present deities from Marilyn to Mao: impassive and cold, totally estranged, in their coloristic intensity they participate in the contemporary imaginative and symbolic universe and increase it. Warhol's is a mythology of second nature—a mythology that—imposing but suspicious of its own self—rises from the late-industrial universe, now mature and accomplished in its changing forms. Beauty, for Warhol—it bears repeating—indeed never coincides with "natural" immediacy, but always derives from an (almost Hegelian) transformation of the first nature: "The red lobster's beauty only comes out when it's dropped into the boiling water . . . and nature changes things and carbon is turned into diamonds and dirt is gold . . . and wearing a ring in your nose is gorgeous."[45] Warhol's new mythological deities are far from any idiosyncratic contraction, foreign to any psychological depth. They decorate the world with their iterative reproposition.

Within this land of forms—which have moved from art to life, inhabiting the contemporary symbolic imagery—beauty has found its place. It has returned, once again, to inhabit this world and, at the same time, it helps to make it habitable. Escaped from the enclosures of aesthetic consciousness, it is once again the measure of the world in this world. It makes it familiar and welcoming. Back to being the (albeit critical) yardstick of the world within the world itself, though in the most critical and sarcastic tones, beauty claims its ancient nature as (probably rightly) free from autonomous art. The aesthetic difference between appearance and reality has really come here to a definite decline. Thus we have reached the furthest borders of the so-called philosophy of art, which for almost two centuries has structured the reflection on art and beauty. This way we have also gone well beyond Platonism, which, as we have seen several times, has dominated philosophical reflection on art since its very beginning.

Thus, from appearance we have turned to nature. But this is not enough: from second nature we go back to the first, thus renewing the solidarity pact that beauty had originally made with the world. Warhol (it's him again, and it's not surprising) writes: "I can never get over when you're on the beach how beautiful the sand looks and the water washes it away and straightens it up and the trees and the grass all look great. I think having land and not ruining it is the most beautiful art that anybody could ever want to own."[46] The melancholic otherness of modern beauty thus disappears from the scene, while its original challenge is renewed again. The world's forms, which beauty earnestly protects, resurface. Warhol thus concludes what, with little respect for history, I have defined "twentieth century."

Classicism, Again

Enlightenment without "Nostos"

So beauty is still here and still constitutes something incontrovertibly necessary. And in many ways, its loss represents the final outcome of a painful journey through (the halls) of a reason that has understood its adulthood in the most drastic way: as a break with its origin. In other words, this reason has no *nostos*, it knows no return, as it is now condemned to travel forever like Wagner's *Flying Dutchman*, unable to find the myth it came from and to which it shall return (to refer to Horkheimer and Adorno's famous statements in their *Dialectic of Enlightenment*).[1] In terms of the journey I have reconstructed in this book, this reason is unable to rise up towards the *eidos*: the form that generated it. It is therefore a model of rationality that, together with its origin, has lost some of its prerogatives, adapting to a path that halves its effectiveness, giving it worth uniquely on the conceptual level.

Upon closer inspection, this reason goes hand in hand with autonomous art, which is the other side of this oblivion of the origin. In fact, in the present, autonomous art represents the residue of the origin (and maybe the nostalgia that much avant-garde had for primitivism actually confirms this hypothesis!). It constitutes the frozen, "anesthetized" face of the image that in the beginning appeared with its majestic power, as evidenced by Hesiod's myth of the birth of Aphrodite. The path of emancipation of the concept thus leaves the image and its intelligence behind.

Having separated the concept from the image, proceeding along a path that severs the subject from the object forever, subjectivity in its active value is embodied by reason, while its passive and objective dimension is attributed to sense data conceived as intuition and imagination. The ancient morphological intelligence—contained by and entrusted to the concept of beauty—has thus disappeared due to a rationality devoted to the beyond, to transcendence, to a formalization that makes it subject to an incessant progress along with the concepts (but only in the sign of receptivity). The beauty that used to dwell in the ambivalent but unambiguous sign of active and passive, and that used to enforce the sovereign subjectivity/objectivity of the image endowed with sparkling attractiveness, is now fully rejected—or, better, it has flown back to the land of ineffectiveness.

Its weakening has even been institutionalized into the museum: it is a sort of symbol of intelligence without *nostos*. It is the treasure chest of memory, which is protected to such an extent that it is locked inside it and unable to exercise any influence over the world. The intelligence of the forms that—as evidenced by the museum—has fallen into a kind of self-referential inefficacy is replaced by a conceptual intelligence that proceeds by casting an unnatural light, without producing shadows that may act as its background, turning into a sort of blinding light. It intends to enlighten everything, at any price, because—in a journey into the unknown where there is no coming back—a deadly threat could be hiding anywhere. It is a terrified reason that we have inherited, one that arrogantly flaunts its need to move forward and hides its helplessness—namely, the fact that it cannot look back.

On the other hand, this reason thinks without the other who is in its background and behind it: it is nondialogical and therefore violent, and must technically impose itself on the world. Moreover, just as it is devoted to a formalized procedure that ensures the world to its categories, it can only be thought of as a technical reason, thus betraying itself and the nature of techne in its intimately poietic quality that does not concern human activity alone.[2] If it were able to get back to itself, it might be able to think about technique not as an antagonist of nature but as something in consonance with it: thus we return to the idea of a "technique of nature" that appeared in the first introduction of the third Kantian critique.[3] Perhaps this way one could also conceive not so much a critique of technological reason but—more articulately—a critique of the bad technique of a bad reason. This would also allow rethinking the essence of technique as something different from a plunge into the totally alienated other. The point is to focus on the technique and rationality of nature. These are tricky issues that have little to do with the classic themes of modern and contemporary aesthetics, such as the autonomy of art or aesthetic disinterest.

Let's try to reduce them to the bone. Why have we come to develop such a devastating technology? Why do we realize only now that we could have proceeded differently? This can possibly be because we haven't given sufficient consideration to that essence of technology to which contemporary thought, from Nietzsche to Heidegger, has outstandingly contributed. In other words, this can be because we have set aside the technical knowledge of nature to embrace a technology that goes against it and destroys it. Isn't this technical knowledge of nature what bears the name of beauty?[4] Perfection of the form that 'thinks' itself as image? This natural intelligence of the forms doesn't share the invasiveness of a disoriented and disorienting intelligence, so unaware of its origin as to have lost its way, unable to even wonder where it really is. Beauty can thus be established as the symbolic image of an Enlightenment that has found or rediscovered the way back, able to look within itself, into its own genetic path.

An "Ecological" Thought

What strategy can we adopt in this context? Let's try to outline it. The starting point would probably be to reverse the Hegelian path—with a degree of respectful irony—and truly go back to Goethe, as I mentioned at the end of my considerations on Andy Warhol in the last chapter. Goethe would undoubtedly have to be translated into the present, understood not literally but spiritually. Let me explain: the point is to find the second nature in the first one (against which Hegel throws a few stones). In other words, it is necessary to recognize the project-like nature of originary nature, which is always already in the process of becoming a second nature. Nature is not an ultimate insurmountable wall, but is always transcending itself.

With respect to the present, this seems to be the most lucid and deepest thing we can learn from Goethe on the unity of art and nature: he speaks of a nature that, in its many forms, is never itself but is always other than itself and beyond itself. From this point of view there is no nature—at least if you understand it as something final. Rather, it is always in becoming. It is the level of forms reaching meaning in the image, allowing for the flourishing of life and human beings as consciously symbolic beings.

This path—which would eventually allow bridging the gap between nature and culture—is also related to art and the central meaning of ornament with which I ended the final chapter. This is because the horizon that has been taking shape has led us far beyond the limits of the idea of autonomous art. In other words, one can speak again of art's effectiveness on the world, regardless of Kant's accusation of ineffectuality followed by its factual sterilization in the closed circuit (effective and powerful in its own way) of the art market.[5] This makes it necessary to speak again of beauty, now that autonomous art has finally disappeared (ideally) with Andy Warhol.

Far from being ineffective, as I said, beauty is an essential need: discovered and rediscovered in its actual scope, it can produce a readaptation of late-modern existence, which is struggling to feel at home in Marc Augé's "non-places."[6] A life conducted in places of passage, airports, highways, and so on is not in itself any less disturbing than the rationalistic "iron cage" within which, according to Max Weber, mature modernity was trapped. Also—to carry on with this slightly rhapsodic list—there is another factor, evident to the point of being trivial: the decorum of existence has been terribly decreasing in the indistinguishable peripheries of our cities, indebted to rationalistic architecture, inspired by a sort of obtuse functionalism that inevitably leads to degradation and the anarchy of abandonment. Isn't this technological catastrophe the telling example of the outcomes of the reason without *nostos*? A reason forced to undertake a journey with no way back, that can only find some familiarity with the world through a universal violent homologation (which goes hand in hand with the increasing social violence)?

These sparse observations should be enough to acknowledge that we could, indeed, use a little beauty. The point would be to replace (as much as possible, of course) the normative rigor of a law perceived as foreign with the objective law of decorum that—also in view of the reference to memory and tradition—raises up existence and gives it context. It's a semantically dense context, acting almost unconsciously over its agents, similarly to what happens with the hermeneutical circle: as is well known, the latter constitutes an intrinsic presupposition to the nature of understanding that is thematized only later.[7] In the case of decorum, as well as in that of the hermeneutical circle, in fact, we have to do with a presupposition that isn't thematized when we are immersed in the respective reference contexts. Let me explain. When we start a novel, we do so while having certain expectations about it, which always remain in the background as we read it; in the same way, the behaviors dictated by a monumental context, in their decorous motions inspired by a desire to improve existence and its style, develop almost automatically, without us needing to understand every single time that some behaviors must fit the place we find ourselves in.

After all, this is how subjects mostly experience art, also in the universe of autonomous art and aesthetic art. Even today, for most people art is still experienced unconsciously, and art has the function of context for the action taking place within it. For example, it is much more frequent that someone would spend time in a town hall, in a church or in a cemetery respectively for bureaucratic, religious, and family reasons compared to the time he or she would spent in an art gallery, experiencing art thematically. In the first cases the individual is simply accompanied by the monumental context, which provides the stage and dictates the behavior to adopt within it. At least when these places perform their function—and do not host, say, a tour—they are not the object of aesthetic conscience.

Did it take a whole book to argue for a pompous return to public art?—you'll say. All of this in defense of decorum and ornaments? Not at all: there is much more: the point is to grasp the issue and the challenge it implies in all its scope. My proposal is rather that of a new conception of classicism, one that is not afraid of the second nature (as opposed to the first) as its background. As I said, this is only possible based on the assumption that nature is always already a second nature, giving itself technically and recognizing itself in the medium of the image. In other words, and following Goethe once again, nature can be known through art. In accordance with his lucid intuition, nature is such only when it exposes on the surface its deep essence and—in this way—communicates itself and its systemic/semantic complexity. The latter is expressed through the form that manages to enclose in a finite structure its infinite components, thus making them intelligible.[8]

It is only by understanding nature this way—recognizing its intrinsic complexity and proximity to significance, which makes it close and familiar to us—that maybe we can truly protect it and avoid the ecological catastrophe we are approaching. Such a disaster is certainly the final outcome of what I have defined "reason without *nostos*," which precluded itself the possibility of self-reflection and of reminding itself where it comes from. The thought of beauty is therefore certainly also an "ecological thought." After all, this is how it becomes possible to take a step back, bridge the gap between the present and the recent past, and go back to Heidegger, adopting the mode of dwelling exposed in "Poetically man dwells."[9] In other words, we must go back to dwelling in the meanings of existence, renewing a condition that allows us to escape the modern and late-modern disorientation. This is the other side of the new monumentality I mentioned above.

However, the point is not to think, in the globalized world of universal homologation, of a new style that would dictate its normative quality in addition to the others. It is rather necessary to intertwine the cultural forms with the living, recognizing in the complexity of the latter a cultured element. It is necessary to find, in the globalized world, the seminatural modalities of an intuitive comprehension of contexts and places. And this of course should happen without giving up the acquired cultural background that translates in the term "complexity." This mode of being and comprehending is deposited in symbolic knowledge as Goethe presented it. As I said, the symbol contemplates infinity in finitude—it reduces complexity without mortifying it. Think, for example, of the famous number 1113 of Goethe's *Maxims and Reflections*: "Symbolism transforms an object of perception into an idea, the idea into an image, and does it in such a way that the idea always remains infinitely operative and unattainable so that even if it is put into words in all languages, it still remains inexpressible."[10]

Therefore the point is to find and renew an intuitive universality rooted in sensibility/intelligibility: that is, in the form. This is what also emerges from the teachings of Edgar Morin, who shows that humans are the only beings that create their own ecosystem. One could say they are the beings whose specificity lies in their immediate grasping of the cultural side of nature: that is, its complexity.[11] But in this way—I'm proceeding in a necessarily rhapsodic manner—one can also refer to some outcomes of neuroscience. Think of the research on mirror neurons, which testify how knowledge follows an imitative pattern that is, broadly speaking, "aesthetic."[12] What is striking is that knowledge itself thus takes on an active attitude for which imitative learning has a performative meaning: it translates into an intersubjectively shared action. Thus it prefigures the idea of intersubjectivity, of community: in short, the inhabitability of the world.

From this point of view, then, one can hypothesize that there is an anthropological necessity of the form: and here the idea of beauty finds its raison d'être, once again. It prefigures a rootedness in the world that at the same time it induces to realize following the folds of the world itself. On the other hand, beauty does not constitute a foundation or a definitive rule but a morphological presupposition that orientates—without dictating them—modalities that reify its being and relativize its cogence rooting it in particular historical and geographical contexts. Therefore, only insofar as beauty conceives of its being as image and not as objective presence—only insofar as it continues to be the presupposition of a recognition and self-recognition that are always yet to come, as the twentieth century has shown—can it pursue its task of nonnormative rule.

In this context one can also recover—without worrying about being trapped by it—what neuroscience told us. For instance, Semir Keki—agreeing with Plato against Plato himself—states that "artists are engaged in a profession that is a search for essential," therefore "the pejorative view expressed by Plato must seem bizarre to them."[13] From this standpoint, art manages to grasp the object in its original morphological quality thanks to which it becomes recognizable as such in all its different modalities and articulations. In short, it is thanks to the artist that we utter the word "dog" when seeing the most diverse kinds and specimen of the species. The formal perfection known as beauty, in this perspective, is the ultimate principle of our dwelling in the world. Without beauty, we could not interpret it.

Notes

Introduction. Beauty and the Twentieth Century

1. Jean Clair begins his *Considérations sur l'État des Beaux-Arts. Critique de la modernité* [Paris: Gallimard, 1983], 9) in a very significant way: "Painting, at the end of this century, is going bad. Those who love the homeland of paintings soon will only have the fence of museums, just as those who love nature are now left with natural reserves, to cultivate their nostalgia of what is no longer there." A similar observation had been made by Zecchi, *La bellezza*, Torino: Bollati Boringhieri, 1990. A fundamental contribution in this sense was given by G. Carchia, *Arte e bellezza. Saggio sull'estetica della pittura* (Bologna: Il Mulino, 1995) which focuses on the modern value of classicism beyond "aesthetic art." Besides, it is no coincidence that the "contemporary relevance of beauty" has recently often appeared also in very popular works. Just to mention some of the books written since year 2000, think of: W. Steiner, *Venus in Exile: The Rejection of Beauty in Twentieth Century Art* (New York: Free Press, 2001); A. Danto, *The Abuse of Beauty: Aesthetics and the Concept of Art* (Chicago: Open Court, 2003); P. Guyer, *Values of Beauty: Historical Essay in Aesthetics* (Cambridge: Cambridge University Press, 2005); C. Sartwell, *Six Names of Beauty* (London: Routledge, 2004); F. Cheng, *Cinq méditations sur la beauté* (Paris, Albin Michel, 2006); A. Nehamas, *Only a Promise of Happiness. The Place of Beauty in a World of Art* (Princeton, NJ: Princeton University Press, 2007); G. Vigarello, *Histoire de la Beauté* (Paris: Seuil, 2004); L. Zoja, *Giustizia e bellezza* (Torino: Bollati Boringhieri, 2007).

2. B. Newman, "The Ides of Art, Six Opinions on What is Sublime in Art?" *Tiger's Eye* 6 (15 December 1948): 52–53.

3. W. Tatarkiewicz, "Beauty: History of the Concept," in *A History of Six Ideas. An Essay in Aesthetics* (New York: Springer, 1980), 121–52; R. Bodei, *Le forme del bello* (Bologna: Il Mulino, 1995).

4. As is known, the idea that myth constitutes a kind of initial "domestication" of nature has been formulated by H. Blumenberg, *Work on Myth* (1979) (Cambridge: MIT Press, 1988), 34ff.

5. Let us not forget that Heaven forced Earth to keep her children inside, while only Aphrodite, free from the suffocating grip, can truly be born and affirm herself as an event, something radically new:

For of all the children that were born of Earth and Heaven, these were the most terrible, and they were hated by their own father from the first. And he used to hide them all away in a secret place of Earth so soon as each was born, and would not suffer them to come up into the light: and Heaven rejoiced in his evil doing. But vast Earth groaned within, being straitened, and she made the element of grey flint and shaped a great sickle, and told her plan to her dear sons. And she spoke, cheering them, while she was vexed in her dear heart: "My children, gotten of a sinful father, if you will obey me, we should punish the vile outrage of your father; for he first thought of doing shameful things." So she said; but fear seized them all, and none of them uttered a word. But great Cronos the wily took courage and answered his dear mother: "Mother, I will undertake to do this deed, for I reverence not our father of evil name, for he first thought of doing shameful things." So he said: and vast Earth rejoiced greatly in spirit, and set and hid him in an ambush, and put in his hands a jagged sickle, and revealed to him the whole plot. And Heaven came, bringing on night and longing for love, and he lay about Earth spreading himself full upon her. Then the son from his ambush stretched forth his left hand and in his right took the great long sickle with jagged teeth, and swiftly lopped off his own father's members and cast them away to fall behind him. And not vainly did they fall from his hand; for all the bloody drops that gushed forth Earth received, and as the seasons moved round she bare the strong Erinyes and the great Giants with gleaming armour, holding long spears in their hands and the Nymphs whom they call Meliae (8) all over the boundless earth. And so soon as he had cut off the members with flint and cast them from the land into the surging sea, they were swept away over the main a long time: and a white foam spread around them from the immortal flesh, and in it there grew a maiden. First she drew near holy Cythera, and from there, afterwards, she came to sea-girt Cyprus, and came forth an awful and lovely goddess, and grass grew up about her beneath her shapely feet. Her gods and men call Aphrodite, and the foam-born goddess and rich-crowned Cytherea, because she grew amid the foam, and Cytherea because she reached Cythera, and Cyprogenes because she was born in billowy Cyprus, and Philommedes (9) because sprang from the members. And with her went Eros, and comely Desire followed her at her birth at the first and as she went into the assembly of the gods. This honour she has from the beginning, and this is the portion allotted to her amongst men and undying gods,—the whisperings of maidens and smiles and deceits with sweet delight and love and graciousness. (Hesiod, *Theogony* [London: William Heinemann, 1914], 89–94)

6. But also in the earlier theory proposed by Democritus; see, in this respect, G. Carchia, *L'estetica antica* (Roma-Bari: Laterza, 1999), 41–45. On ancient aesthetics

in general see also: E. Grassi, *Arte come antiarte. Saggio sulla teoria del bello nel mondo antico* (Torino: Paravia, 1972); W. Tatarkiewicz, *Ancient Aesthetics*, reprint (Berlin: de Gruyter, 1970); G. Lombardo, *L'estetica antica* (Bologna: Il Mulino, 2002).

7. R. Bodei, "La bellezza del mondo," in *Le forme del bello*, 17–33.

8. Plato, *Plato in Twelve Volumes*, trans. W.R.M. Lamb, vol. 9 (Cambridge, MA: Harvard University Press,1925), *Timaeus*, 30b and 30d.

9. Ibid., *Hippias Major*, 288a.

10. Plato. *Plato in Twelve Volumes*, trans. P. Shorey, vols. 5 and 6 (Cambridge, MA: Harvard University Press, 1969), *Republic*, 598b.

11. See chapter 4.

12. For more on the aesthetic issue in Middle Ages, see: W. Tatarkiewicz, *Medieval Aesthetics* (Mouton De Gruyter, 1971); U. Eco, *Arte e bellezza nell'estetica medievale* (Milano: Bompiani, 1987), in particular, with regards to beauty as a transcendental, 25–38; M. Fumagalli Beonio Brocchieri, *L'estetica medieval* (Bologna: Il Mulino, 2002).

13. Here I am referring to the topic and title of O. Marquard, *Aesthetica und Anaesthetica* (München: Fink, 2003). A fundamental work to analyze the rise of aesthetic consciousness and it meaning is H.G. Gadamer, *Truth and Method* (London: Bloomsbury Academic, 2004), 3ff., especially the sections beginning at 37 and 70.

14. A quite recent and comprehensive analysis of the issue can be found in the collection of essays *Dopo il museo*, edited by F. Luisetti and G. Maragliano (Turin: Trauben, 2006).

15. [G.W.F. Hegel?, F.W.J. Schelling?, and F. Hölderlin?], "The Oldest Systematic Program of German Idealism," in *The Early Political Writings of The German Romantics*, edited by F.C. Beiser (Cambridge, MA: Cambridge University Press 1966), 4.

16. F. Schlegel, *On the Study of Greek Poetry* (New York: SUNY Press, 2001), 18–19.

17. G.W.F. Hegel, *Aesthetics. Lectures on Fine Art*, translated by T.M. Knox, 2 vols. (Oxford: Clarendon Press, 1975).

18. Ibid., 1.

19. Hegel's phrasing is here absolutely exemplary, in that art is thus deprived of its truth and definitively transferred to the sphere of appearance. In this regard, see Hegel, *Aesthetics*, I: 119–20.

20. This is true regardless of the fact that in some important occasions it is still extensively considered, albeit significantly circumventing its transcendent meaning. This, for example, took place at the turn of the new century with a thinker such as George Santayana, who defines aesthetic pleasure as resulting from the beauty subsisting in things: *The Sense of Beauty. Being the Outlines of Aesthetic Theory* (New York: Charles Scribner's Sons, 1896).

21. Nehamas, *Only a Promise of Happiness*.

22. To refer to the title and topic of one of the first books of the group of the School of Constance coordinated by Hans Robert Jauss, "Poetik und Hermeneutik":

H.R. Jauss (editor), *Die nicht mehr schöne Kunste: Grenzphänomene des Ästhetischen* (München: Fink, 1968).

23. For more on this, see for instance P. D'Angelo, *Estetismo* (Bologna: Il Mulino, 2003), esp. 85–109 (*Dandy*).

24. H. Broch, "Kitsch" (1933) and "Notes on the Problem of Kitsch" (1950) in *Kitsch: The World of Bad Taste* ed. G. Dorfles (New York: Bell Publishing, 1969).

25. See in this respect, P. Bürger, *Theory of the Avant-garde* (Manchester: Manchester University Press 1984), esp. 15–34 ("Theory of the Avant-Garde and Critical Literary Science").

26. This happens after all even when beauty takes on—as in futurism—an ambiguously objective feature. In this case one can see unstable beauty, crossed by time, the new form of transcendence. It is almost superfluous to mention in this context the famous peroration of a new beauty, built in the name of speed, made by Marinetti in the first futurist manifesto: "We affirm that the world's magnificence has been enriched by a new beauty: the beauty of speed. A racing car whose hood is adorned with great pipes, like serpents of explosive breath—a roaring car that seems to ride on grapeshot is more beautiful than the Victory of Samothrace." F.T. Marinetti, "The Founding and Manifesto of Futurism" (first published in *Le Figaro* [February 20, 1909]) in *Documents of 20th Century Art: Futurist Manifestos*, ed. U. Apollonio, and trans. R. Brain, R.W. Flint, J.C. Higgitt, and C. Tisdall (New York: Viking Press, 1973), 19–24.

27. On this topic, I refer the reader to my *Introduzione al nichilismo* (Roma-Bari: Laterza, 1992), 56ff.

28. E. Bloch, *The Spirit of Utopia* (Stanford, CA: Stanford University Press, 2000), 27.

29. A. Danto, "The Philosopher as Andy Warhol," in *Philosophizing Art. Selected Essays* (Los Angeles: University of California Press, 1999), 61–83.

30. A. Danto, *Beyond the Brillo Box. The Visual Arts in Post-historical Perspective* (Los Angeles: University of California Press, 1992), 139.

31. In this regard, especially as for the destiny of public art (on which I return in the conclusions), see F. Duque, *Abitare la terra. Ambiente, umanismo, città* (Bergamo: Moretti & Vitali, 2007).

Chapter I. The Romantic Farewell to Beauty

1. F. Nietzsche, *The Gay Science* (Leipzig: E.W. Fritzsch, 1887), 181.

2. In this regard, see the critical observations by K.H. Bohrer, "Il fantastico romantico come coscienza decentrata," in *Romanticismo e Modernità*, ed. C. Ciancio and F. Vercellone (Turin: Zamorani, 1996), 119–41.

3. F. Schlegel, *Kritische Friedrich-Schlegel-Ausgabe*, ed. E. Behler in collaboration with J.-J. Anstett and H. Eichner, 22 vols. ([München: Schöningh/Thomas,

1962–2006], 18: 81 [619]). Hereafter I shall refer to this edition as *KA* followed by the volume number, the page number, and the indication of the fragment.

4. This path will find its fulcrum in Novalis, thus constituting a kind of unresolved polarity within the Frühromantik. In this regard, allow me to refer to my *Nature del tempo. Novalis e la forma poetica del romanticismo tedesco* (Milano: Guerini, 1998), and in particular to chapter 3, "Moralizzazione della Natura," 83–127.

5. J.W. Goethe, "Einwirkung Der Neueren Philosophie," *Erstdruck: Zur Morphologie* I:2 (1820).

6. As is known, the Platonic revival is a fundamental moment in German culture in the 1790s. Think of the works of D. Tiedemann, *Geist der spekulativen Philosophie* (Marburg: Neue Akademische Buchhandlung, 1791–92); W.G. Tennemann, *Grundriss der Geschichte der Philosophie*, 12 vols. (Leipzig: Barth, 1798–1819), up until Friedrich Schlegel and Schleiermacher's common project to publish Plato in German (this project failed because of Schlegel and was later completed by Schleiermacher alone). On Plato in Romanticism see the seminal studies of: W. Beierwaltes, *Platonismus und Idealismus* (Frankfurt: Klostermann, 1972); H. Krämer, *Plato and the Foundations of Metaphysics: A Work on the Theory of the Principles and Unwritten Doctrines of Plato with a Collection of the Fundamental Documents* (New York: SUNY Press, 1990); H. Krämer, *Il paradigma romantico nell'interpretazione di Platone* (Napoli: Istituto Suor Orsola Benincasa, 1991). Thanks to Plato, Schlegel's thought acquires a degree of progressiveness, as noted by E. Behler in the "Einleitung" to the "Philosophische Lehrjahre," in *KA*, 18: xii (ss). This makes his proposal very different from Schleiermacher's.

7. This trend can be found not only in Schlegel, but also in Niethammer's *Philosophisches Journal einer Gesellschaft teutscher Gelehrten*. In this regard, see especially M. Frank, "Philosophische Grundlagen der Frühromantik," in *Athenäum. Jahrbuch für Romantik*, (1994), 4: 37–130; M. Frank, "Ogni verità è relativa, ogni sapere simbolico. Motivi dello scetticismo nei confronti del principio fondamentale nel primo romanticismo jenese (1796)," in *Romanticismo e modernità*, ed. J. Ciancio and F. Vercellone, (Turin: Zamorani, 1996), 47–74. For a comprehensive overview of the matter, see E. Behler, *Unendliche Perfektibilität. Europäische Romantik und Französische Revolution* (Paderborn: Schöningh, 1989).

8. *KA*, 11: 120.

9. H. Belting, *Das unsichtbare Meisterwerk* (München: Beck, 1998), offers a lucid analysis on the relation between art and the ideal, understood as a paradigm of modern art. However, he doesn't relate this to the Platonic revival in Germany at the end of the eighteenth century.

10. See Friedrich Schlegel's review, "[Über] Esquisse d'un tableau historique des progrès de l'esprit humain. Ouvrage posthume de [1795]," first published in *Philosophisches Journal einer Gesellschaft teutscher Gelehrten* 3:2 (1795): 161–72 (reprinted [Hildesheim: Olms, 1969], now also in *KA*, 7: 3–10).

11. *KA*, 23: 129–30.

12. Suffice it to recall in this context the project of a morphology as it is formulated by Goethe in a short paper dated 1807:

Scientific men at all times have displayed a drive to comprehend living forms as such, to grasp the connections of their external visible and tangible parts as indicative of the internal parts, and so to control the whole, to a certain extent, in an intuitive perception [*Anschauung*]. How close this scientific urge is conceited to the artistic and imitative drive we need not go into. One finds thus in the course of art, of knowledge, and of science several attempts to ground and develop a doctrine, which we would like to call morphology. [. . .] To indicate the overall existence of a real being, the German uses the word *Gestalt*, form: in this term we abstract from what is mobile, and we establish a single whole, taken as completed and set in its characters. Now, if we examine the existing forms, but especially the organisms, we shall see that in them there is never anything immobile, fixed, completed, but everything sways in a continuous motion. So the German appropriately uses the word *Bildung*, formation, to indicate both what is produced, and what is being produced. It follows that, in an introduction to morphology, one should not speak of the form. [. . .] The already formed is immediately transformed again; and if we want to gain a living perception of nature, we too have to keep mobile and plastic following the example that it gives us. (J.W. Goethe, "Die Absicht Eingeleitet" [1807] in his *Zur Morphologie* 1:1, as collected in *Goethe. Die Schriften zure Naturwissenschaft,* 1st division, vol. 9, ed. Dorothea Kuhn [Weimar: Bohlaus Nachfolger, 1954], 7.)

13. The "extreme" character of the Romantic project of the total book, a challenge to the nominalism characteristic of the *Moderne*, is underlined by H. Blumenberg, *Die Lesbarkeit der Welt* (Frankfurt: Suhrkamp, 1979): "That a 'novel' about the universe could be conceived reveals the ever-transgressive trend of the genre as much as the need of the time to express itself in it. [. . .] The peculiar availability of what had not yet turned into a scientific discipline promotes the open consistency of the concept of reality which underpins the novel. One could refer analogously to the totalizing claim of the French Encyclopaedia—with its indecision between final account of the whole of human performance and the foundation of the future as the set of possibilities that this entails."

14. G.W.F. Hegel, *Aesthetics. Lectures on Fine Art,* trans. T.M. Knox, vol. 1 (Oxford: Clarendon Press, 1975), 75, 517ff.

15. *KA,* 18: 11 (79).

16. *KA,* 18: 20–21 (25).

17. Hegel, *Aesthetics,* vol. 1, 11.

18. In regards to this crucial passage, see P. Szondi, "Antico e moderno nell'estetica dell'età di Goethe," in *Poetica e filosofia della storia,* eds. R. Gilodi and F. Vercellone

(Turin: Einaudi, 2001), 165ff. As regards the centrality of "feeling" to eighteenth-century aesthetics, see E. Franzini, *L'estetica del Settecento* (Bologna: Il Mulino, 1995).

19. J.J. Winckelmann, *Reflections on the Painting and Sculpture of the Greeks* (London: A. Millar, 1765), 30.

20. See P. Szondi, *Poetica e filosofia della storia*, 203–05.

21. R. Arnheim, *Entropy and Art* (Berkeley: University of California Press, 1971), 21–22.

22. In this regard, allow me to refer to my "Il desiderio nel romanticismo tedesco," in *Morfologie del moderno. Saggi di ermeneutica dell'immagine* (Genova: Il Melangolo, 2006), 116–30. About the onset of chaos in modern art, see the fundamental essay by H. Sedlmayr, *Verlust der Mitte: die bildenden Kunst des 19. und 20. Jahrhunderts als Symptom und Symbol der Zeit* (Salzburg: Müller, 1948), in particular 10–137.

23. This is also noted, in a different context, by Belting, *Das unsichtbare Meisterwerk* (München: Beck, 1998), 28–32.

24. Ibid., 32–36.

25. I cannot focus here on the topic of "degenerate art" and on the cultural policy of national socialism in relation to the arts. In this regard, see Hitler's speech of 1937, with which the Führer inaugurates the Große Deutsche Kunst-Ausstellung 1937, which was opened in Monaco before that of "Entartete Kunst," of "degenerate art": "Der Führer eröffnet die Große Deutsche Kunstausstellung 1937," in *Die Kunst im Dritten Reich* I, 7/8 (1937): 47–61. For the reference to the 'German' theme in art, not only in the field of national socialism, see. H. Belting, *Die Deutschen und ihre Kunst* (Munich: Beck, 1992). Regarding the union of Greece and Germany as the foundation of an improbable national socialist revival of classicism, see. A. Bäumler, "Hellas und Germanien (1937)," in *Studien zur deutschen Geistesgeschichte* (Berlin: Junker und Dünnhaupt, 1943), 295–311.

26. In this case, in a mystical key, as evidenced for example in the following passage: "If you want to show what you see it is necessary for you to look away from art and focus on nature. [. . .] So if you want to wander with me in the splendour of phenomena and look at the things God has created, you shall know what you see, and the light of your bedroom shall not burn without you joyfully sensing the close presence of your God" (P.O. Runge, *Farbenkugel* [Hamburg: Bey Friedrich Perthes, 1810], 3).

27. On this topic, see especially the famous essay by O.F. Bollnow, "Was heisst, einen Schriftsteller besser verstehen, als er sich selber verstanden hat?," in *Das Verstehen. Drei Aufsätze zur Theorie der Geisteswissenschaften* (Mainz: Kirckheim & Co., 1949), 7–33. See also T. Griffero, "Ciò che l'autore non sa. Su una formula tradizionale dell'ermeneutica," in *Ciò che l'autore non sa: ermeneutica, tradizione, critica*, ed. E. Franzini, M. Ferraris, T. Griffero, and F. Vercellone (Milano: Guerini e Associati, 1988), 9–34.

28. F. Schlegel, "On Incomprehensibility," in *F. Schlegel's Lucinde and the Fragments* (Minneapolis: University of Minnesota Press, 1971), 268.

29. For an overview of the contrast between design and color in the perspective that interests us here, see D. Riout, *Qu'est-ce que l'art modern?* (Paris: Gallimard, 2000).

30. For the renewed popularity of this formula, see M. Cometa, *L'età di Goethe* (Roma:, Carocci, 2006);[2] and, regarding the idea of a new Renaissance, see M. Fuhrmans, *Schellings Philosophie der Weltalter: Schellings Philosophie in den Jahren 1806–1821. Zum Problem des Schellingschen Theismus* (Düsseldorf: Schwann, 1954), in particular, chap. I.

31. As for Romantic nihilism, I would refer the reader to the first chapter of my *Introduzione al nichilismo* (Roma Bari: Laterza, 1992), 2005,[7] 3–30.

32. As for the avant-garde's aspiration to rejoin life, see P. Bürger, *Theorie der Avantgarde* (Frankfurt: Suhrkamp, 1974).

Chapter II. The Non-containing Form: From Nietzsche to Spengler

1. See G. Boehm, ed., B*eschreibungskunst—Kunstbeschrei-bung: Ekphrasis von der Antike bis zur Gegenwart* (München: Fink, 1995).

2. See T. Mann, *Reflections of a Non-Political Man* (New York: Frederick Ungar, 1983). For a comprehensive look at the relationship between philosophy and the novel, see the seminal study by S. Givone, *Il bibliotecario di Leibniz. Filosofia e romanzo* (Torino: Einaudi, 2005).

3. G. Lukács, *The Theory of the Novel* (London: Merlin Press, 1963).

4. Aristotle, *Poetics* (New York: Penguin Classics, 1996).

5. On this, see for instance R. Nöthlich "Wissenschaftspopulari-sierung im Umfeld—Der Zoologe und Verleger Wilhelm Breitenbach," in *Klassische Universität und akade- mische Provinz. Die Universität Jena des 19. Jahrhundert bis in die 30er Jahre des 20. Jahrhunderts,* eds. M. Steinbach and S. Gerber (Jena: Bussert & Stadeler Verlag, 2004).

6. In this regard, see especially E. Haeckel, *Kunstformen der Natur* (1904), *Die einhundert Tafeln,* with a commentary by R.P. Hartmann and contributions by O. Breidbach and I. Eibl-Eibesfeldt (München: Prestel, 1998).

7. I refer the reader to O. Breidbach, M. Di Bartolo, and F. Vercellone, "La seppia e il sublime. Note sulla naturalizzazione dell'estetica contemporanea," in *Estetica* 2 (2004): 5–32.

8. For a more exhaustive discussion, see my "Cristianesimo senza mito? Da Nietzsche a Girard," now in *Morfologie del moderno. Saggi di ermeneutica dell'immagine,* ed. F. Vercellone (Genova: Il Melangolo, 2006), 149–62.

9. See *The Complete Works of Friedrich Nietzsche* (Stanford, CA: Stanford University Press, 1995).

10. F. Nietzsche, "A Letter to My Friend in Which I Recommend that He Read My Favorite Poet (19 October 1861)," in *Selected Letters of Friedrich Nietzsche,* ed. C. Middleton (Cambridge: Hackett, 1996). 4.

11. F. Nietzsche, *The Anti-Christ, Ecce Homo, Twilight of the Idols* (Cambridge: Cambridge University Press, 2005), xxvi. On Hölderlin and Nietzsche see: A. Negri, "Hölderlin, Nietzsche e la 'Histoire,'" in *Giornale critico della filosofia italiana* 44 (1965): 198–229; V. Vivarelli, "Empedocle e Zarathustra: dissipazione di ricchezza e voluttà del tramonto. Gli echi delle letture hölderliniane in 'Così parlò Zarathustra,'" in *La "Biblioteca ideale" di Nietzsche*, eds. G. Campioni and A. Venturelli (Napoli: Guida, 1992), 201–35; V.L. Waibel, "Hölderlin und Nietzsche über Philistertum und wahre Bildung," in *Nietzsche-Forschung. Jahrbuch der Nietzsche-Gesellschaft* 11 (2004): 45–62.

12. F. Nietzsche, "Aus meimem Leben" (1863), in *Werke in drei Bänden* (München: Karl Hanser, 1954), 3:107.

13. See F.W.J. Schelling, "Timaeus," in *Epoché: A Journal for the History of Philosophy* 12 (Spring 2008): 205–48.

14. On this, see *On the Use and Abuse of History for Life*: http://la.utexas.edu/users /hcleaver/330T/ 350kPEENietzscheAbuseTableAll.pdf: "The culture of a people, in contrast to that barbarism, was once described (and correctly so, in my view) as a unity of the artistic style in all expressions of the life of the people. [. . .] The people to whom we ascribe a culture should be only in a really vital unity and not so miserably split apart into inner and outer, into content and form" (15).

15. F. Nietzsche, *The Antichrist* (New York: Alfred A. Knopf, 1918), par. 16.

16. See J. Taubes, "Die Rechtfertigung des Hässlichen im urchristlicher Tradition," in *Vom Kult zur Kultur* (München: Fink, 1996).

17. F. Nietzsche, *The Will to Power (Notes written 1883–1888)*, bk. 4, no. 1066, trans. W. Kaufmann and R.J. Hollingdale and ed. W. Kaufmann (New York: Vintage Books, 1968), 549.

18. Ibid., 544.

19. On Nietzsche and German expressionism, also starting from the theme of the "naked man," see F. Masini, *Lo scriba del caos. Interpretazione di Nietzsche* (Bologna: Il Mulino, 1978); F. Masini, *Il travaglio del disumano. Per una fenomenologia del nichilismo* (Napoli: Bibliopolis, 1982).

20. J.W. Goethe:

Die Morphologie soll die Lehre von der Gestalt, der Bildung und Umbildung der organischen Körper enthalten; sie gehört daher zu den Naturwissenschaften, deren besondere Zwecke wir nunmehr durchgehen. Die Naturgeschichte nimmt die mannigfaltige Gestalt der organischen Wesen als ein bekanntes Phänomen an. (*Betrachtung* über *Morphologie* überhaupt. *Werke, Kommentare und Register* [Hamburger: Ausgabe in 14 Bänden, Band 13, Hamburg: Wegner, 1966] (5 ed.), 114.)

21. Ibid.
22. Ibid., 123–24.

23. J.W. Goethe, *Studie nach Spinoza*, 7–8.

24. Ibid., 56.

25. Ibid., 17–18.

26. *Der Briefwechsel zwischen Schiller und Goethe nach den Handschriften des Goethe- und Schiller-Archivs*, 3 vols., ed. H.G. Gräf and A. Leitzmann (Leipzig: Insel, 1965), I: 399 (291).

27. E. Haeckel, *Generelle Morphologie der Organismen*, vol. 1 (1866; repr., Berlin: de Gruyter, 1988), 6.

28. Ibid., 5.

29. Ibid., 6.

30. Ibid.

31. Ibid., 7.

32. O. Breidbach, and E. Haeckel, *Bildwelten der Natur* (München: Prestel, 2006), in particular 253–64.

33. C. Middleton, ed., *Selected Letters of Friedrich Nietzsche* (Indianapolis, IN: Hackett Publishing, 1996), 41.

34. As for the ambivalent structure of Dilthey's aesthetics, always oscillating between structure and individuality, see F. Rodi, *Morphologie und Hermeneutik. Zur Methode von Diltheys Ästhetik* (Stuttgart: Kohlhammer, 1969).

35. W. Dilthey, "Construction of the Historical World," in *Dilthey: Selected Writings* (Cambridge, MA: Cambridge University Press 1976), 198.

36. Ibid., 199.

37. On this, see R. Gilodi, *Una vita in forma di libro. Ermeneutica e romanzo tra Illuminismo e Romanticismo* (Genova: Il Melangolo, 2005).

38. On this, see G. Matteucci, "L'esperienza estetica in Wilhelm Dilthey," introduction to W. Dilthey, *Estetica e Poetica* (Milano: Angeli, 1992), esp. 28–46.

39. W. Dilthey, "Die Entstehung der Hermeneutik. Zusätze aus den Handschriften," in *Gesammelte Schriften*, vol. 5, *Die geistige Welt. Einleitung in die Philosophie des Lebens, erste Hälfte, Abhandlungen zur Grundlegung der Geistewissenschaften* (Stuttgart: Vandenhoeck and Ruprecht, 1957), 335.

40. In this context one must surely not forget the conference "Nietzsche und sein Jahrhundert. Rede gehalten am 15. Oktober 1924, dem 80. Geburtstage Nietzsches," in *Reden und Aufsätze*, ed. O. Spengler (München: Beck, 1937), esp. 110–11, where Spengler highlights the Nietzschean but also Goethean elements of his thought.

41. As regards the turn of hermeneutics away from morphology, see the introduction to Rodi, *Morphologie und Hermeneutik*.

42. O. Spengler, *The Decline of the West* (New York: Albert Knopf, 1926), 7. I shall henceforth refer to this text as *DW*, followed by the page number.

43. As already testified at the time by texts such as M. Schröter, *Der Streit um Spengler. Kritik seiner Kritiker* (München, Beck, 1922). See also the seminal study A. Mohler, *Die konservative Revolution in Deutschland 1918–1932*, 3rd ed. (Darmstadt: Wissenschaftliche Buchgesellschaft, 1989); M. Nacci, *Tecnica e cultura della crisi*

1914–1939 (Torino: Loescher, 1982); J. Herf, *Il modernismo reazionario. Tecnologia, cultura e politica nella Germania di Weimar e del terzo Reich* (Bologna: Il Mulino, 1988); A. Demandt and J. Farrunkopf, eds., *Der Fall Spenglers. Eine kritische Bilanz* (Köln: Böhlau, 1994); R.P. Sieferle, *Die konservative Revolution. Fünf biographische Skizzen*, ed. Paul Lensch, Werner Sombart, Oswald Spengler, Ernst Jünger, Hans Freyer) (Frankfurt am Main: Fischer, 1995); B. Beßlich, *Faszination des Verfalls: Thomas Mann und Oswald Spengler* (Berlin: Akademie, 2002).

44. *DW*, 4.

45. For the historical roots of the matter, see B.A. Sørensen, *Symbol und Symbolismus in den ästhetischen Theorien des 18. Jahrhunderts und der deutschen Romantik* (Copenhagen: Munskgaard, 1963).

46. *DW*, 129.

47. See *DW*, 141.

48. On this, see for instance *DW*, 181ff. and chapter 3 of this book, devoted to Bloch. See also E. Bloch, "The Production of the Ornament," in *The Spirit of Utopia* (Stanford, CA: Stanford University Press, 2000), 10–33. It would be of particular interest to compare the anticlassicism of the two and their respective opinions on the Egyptian world and Greek culture to probably derive a stable cultural model beyond ideological disposition. For the Gothic style in the vanguard and its late eighteenth-century roots I refer the reader to my "Arte e mondo dell'espressione da Goethe al 'Blauer Reiter,'" in *Bios e anthropos. Filosofia, biologia e antropologia*, ed. G.F. Frigo (Milano: Guerini, 2007), 33–50.

49. On this, see J. Moltmann, *The Trinity and the Kingdom of God* (Minneapolis, MI: Fortress Press, 1993).

50. Ovid, *Metamorphosis* 6: vv, 1145.

51. Paul, *The Epistle to the Philippians*, II: 67.

52. *DW*, 305.

53. It is almost superfluous to refer to the very famous passage of the introduction to Hegel's *Aesthetics*:

But just as art has its "before" in nature and the finite spheres of life, so too it has an "after," i.e., a region which in turn transcends art's *way* of apprehending and representing the Absolute. For art has still a limit in itself and therefore passes over into higher forms of consciousness. This limitation determines, after all, the position which we are accustomed to assign to art in our contemporary life. For us art counts no longer as the highest mode in which truth fashions an existence for itself. (102)

54. *DW*, 168.

55. See *DW*, 161ff.

56. *DW*, 252.

57. *DW*, 262.

Chapter III. From Modernity to the Avant-Garde

1. J.G. Herder, "*Von deutscher Art und Kunst*," in *Schriften zur Ästhetik und Literatur 1767–1781*, ed. G.E. Grimm (Frankfurt am Main: Deutscher Klassiker Verlag, 1993), 443–562.

2. J.W. Goethe, *Goethe's Literary Essays*, ed. J.E. Spingarn (New York: Harcourt, Brace and Company, 1921), 9.

3. L. Bendavid, *Ueber griechische und gothische Baukunst*, in *Die Horen. Eine Monatsschrift* 3 (1795), 8:87–102 (repr., Darmstadt: Wissenschftliche Buchgesellschaft, 1959), http://www.ub.uni- bielefeld.de/diglib/aufkl/ horen/horen.htm.

4. H. Wölfflin, *Principles of Art History: The Problem Of The Development Of Style In Later Art* (New York: Dover Publications, 1950).

5. Goethe, *Goethe's Literary Essays*, 7.

6. J. Derrida, *The Truth in Painting* (Chicago: Chicago University Press, 1987).

7. W.H. Wackenroder, *Confessions and Fantasies* (University Park: Pennsylvania State University, 1971), 170.

8. W. Morris, *Architecture, Industry and Wealth* (London: Longmans Press, 1902), 88.

9. Ibid., 101.

10. J. Ruskin, *The Stones of Venice*, ed. J.G. Links (New York: Da Capo, 1960), 160.

11. Ibid., 177.

12. Ibid., 175–76.

13. W. Kandinski and F. Marc, eds., *The Blaue Reiter Almanac*, New Documentary Edition, (London: Thames and Hudson, 1974). For the meaning of popular art in *Blauer Reiter*, see J. Hülsewig-Johnen, ed., *Der Blaue Reiter. Avantgarde und Volkskunst. Sammlung Hertha Koenig* (Bielefeld: Medien, 2003). As for the influence of the "art of the primitives," see M. Passaro, "L'almanacco è diventato il nostro sogno," introduction to A. Macke and F. Marc, *Il nostro sogno. Lettere 1910–1914*, ed. M. Passaro (Milano: Mimesis, 2006), esp. 21–30.

14. Ibid., 85.

15. Ibid., 89.

16. Macke, "Die Masken," in *Der Blaue Reiter*, 79. This passage doesn't appear in the English translation.

17. For example, Marc states: "There is only one thing that is not altogether nature, but rather the overcoming and interpreting of nature: art. Art always has been and is in its very essence the boldest departure from nature and 'naturalness.' It is the bridge into the spirit world . . . the necromancy of human race." (Quoted in P. Selz, *German Expressionist Painting* [Berkeley: University of California Press, 1974], 210.)

18. W. Kandinsky, "On the Question of Form," in *Theories of Modern Art: A Source Book by Artists and Critics*, ed. H.B. Chipp, P. Selz, J.C. Taylor (Berkeley: University of California Press, 1968), 155.

19. Ibid., 164.

20. P. Klee, *Paul Klee Notebooks,* ed. J. Spiller, vol. 1 (London: Lund Humphries, 1961), 89.

21. These essays are now collected in W. Worringer, *Fragen und Gegenfragen* (München: Piper, 1956).

22. W. Worringer, *Zur Frage der gotischen Monumentalität* (München: Piper, 1956), 44.

23. W. Worringer, *Spätgotisches und expressionistisches Formsystem* (München: Piper, 1956), 73.

24. Ibid., 75.

25. Ibid., 76–77.

26. O. Spengler, *The Decline of the West* (hereafter *DW*), 175.

27. *DW*, 68.

28. Ibid., 187.

29. Ibid.

30. Ibid., 59.

31. Ibid., 66ff.

32. Ibid., 193.

33. Bloch, *The Spirit of Utopia*, 22.

34. Ibid., 24.

35. Ibid., 26.

36. Ibid., 27.

37. P. Bürger, *Theory of the Avant-Garde* (Minneapolis: University of Minnesota Press, 1984).

38. B. Croce, *Aesthetic As Science Of Expression And General Linguistic* (London: Macmillan & Co., 1909), 13.

39. Ibid., 26.

40. Ibid., 129.

41. Ibid., 129–30.

42. Ibid., 132.

43. This 'ancient' historiographic category was recently taken up by M. Cometa, *L'età di Goethe* (Roma: Carocci, 2006).

44. On this, see P. Szondi, "Antico e moderno nell'estetica dell'età di Goethe," in *Poetica e filosofia della storia*, ed. R. Gilodi and F. Vercellone (Torino: Einaudi, 2001), 163–381.

45. Croce is peremptory in this regard: "Not only is the art of savages not inferior, as art, to that of civilized peoples, provided it be correlative to the impressions of the savage; but every individual, indeed every moment of the spiritual life of an individual, has its artistic world; and all those worlds are, artistically, incomparable with one another." (*Aesthetic*, 226.)

46. Ibid., 229–30.

47. Ibid., 201.

48. Ibid., 249.

49. B. Croce, *La poesia* (Bari: Laterza, 1953[5]), 8.

50. Ibid., 18–19.

51. Ibid., 81–82.

52. Ibid., 120–21.

53. Ibid., 125.

Chapter IV. From Negativity to the Event: Adorno after Heidegger

1. F. Schlegel, "Lyceum Fragments," in *Lucinde and the Fragments* (Minneapolis: University of Minnesota Press, 1971), 144.

2. T. Adorno, *Negative Dialectics*, trans. Dennis Redmond, (2001), 4, http:// members.efn.org/~dredmond/ ndintro.PDF.

3. Ibid., 21.

4. Ibid., 10.

5. To take up the category elaborated by O. Marquard, *Aesthetica und Anaesthetica* (München: Fink, 2003).

6. See for instance T. Adorno, *Aesthetic Theory* (London: Continuum, 1997).

7. Adorno, *Negative Dialectics*, 7.

8. Ibid., 10.

9. K. Rosenkranz, *Aesthetics of Ugliness* (London: Bloomsbury, 2015).

10. Adorno, *Aesthetic Theory*, 48–49.

11. Ibid., 52.

12. Ibid., 102.

13. Ibid., 39.

14. As is well known, the comparison between Heidgger and Adorno was started by H. Mörchen, *Macht und Herrschaft im Denken von Heidegger und Adorno* (Stuttgart: Klett-Cotta, 1980); H. Mörchen, *Adorno und Heidegger. Untersuchung einer philosophischen Kommunika- tionsweigerung* (Stuttgart: Klett-Cotta, 1981). The theme of this comparison, productive in spite of the distance between the two, was resumed also recently. See *Adorno e Heidegger. Soggettività, arte, esistenza*, ed. L. Cortella, M. Ruggenini, and A. Bellan (Roma: Donzelli, 2005). On the issue, see also G. Seubold, *Das Ende der Kunst und der Paradigmenwechsel in der Ästhetik. Philosophische Untersuchungen zu Adorno, Heidegger und Gehlen in systematischer Absicht* (Freiburg-München: Alber, 1997).

15. W. Benjamin, *Illuminations* (New York: Houghton Mifflin Harcourt, 1968), 225.

16. W. Benjamin, *The Arcades Project* (Cambridge, MA: Harvard University Press, 2002).

17. W. Benjamin, *Illuminations*, 239.

18. See in this regard G. Vattimo, "L'arte dell'oscillazione," in *La società trasparente* (Milano: Garzanti, 1989), 63–83, in particular 74ff.

19. T. Adorno, *The Jargon of Authenticity* (Evanston, IL: Northwestern University Press, 1973).

20. In this respect, I refer the reader to my *Introduzione al nichilismo* (Roma-Bari: Laterza, 1992), 112–28.

21. On this, see my "Heidegger e Bäumler interpreti di Nietzsche," in *Metafisica e nichilismo. Löwith e Heidegger interpreti di Nietzsche*, ed. C. Gentili, W. Stegmaier, and A. Venturelli (Bologna: Pendragon, 2006), 223–34.

22. M. Heidegger, "European Nihilism," in *Nietzsche, IV: Nihilism*, ed. D.F. Krell (New York: Harper & Row, 1982), 8.

23. M. Heidegger, "Zu Ernst Jünger," in *Gesamtausgabe*, ed. P. Trawny, vol. 4, band 90 (Frankfurt am Main: Klostermann, 2004), 365.

24. Ibid., 264.

25. E. Jünger, Über *die Linie* (Frankfurt am Main: Klostermann, 1952), 20.

26. Ibid., § 20–21.

27. M. Heidegger, "Uber 'die Linie,'" in *Zur Seinsfrage* (Frankfurt am Main, Klostermann, 1959), 40.

28. M. Heidegger, *Off the Beaten Track* (Cambridge, MA: Cambridge University Press, 2002), 1.

29. Ibid., 46–47, 49.

Chapter V. The Dissolution of the Artwork
and the Rebirth of Ancient Beauty

1. See in this respect the seminal study by A. Béguin, *L'âme romantique et le rêve, essai sur le romantisme allemand et la poésie française* (Marseille: Cahiers du Sud, 1937). M. Heidegger, "European Nihilism," in *Nietzsche, IV: Nihilism*, ed. David F. Krell (New York, Harper & Row, 1982), 8.

2. F. Alquié, *Philosophie du surréalisme* (Paris: Flammarion, 1955), 10.

3. Ibid., 15–16.

4. Ibid., 16–17.

5. Ibid., 24.

6. P. Waldberg, *Surrealism* (Oxford: Oxford University Press, 1978), 16.

7. Ibid., 66.

8. Ibid.

9. Alquié, *Philosophie du surréalisme*, 191–92.

10. Ibid., 195.

11. M. Filoni, *Il filosofo della domenica. La vita e il pensiero di Alexandre Kojève* (Torino: Bollati Boringhieri, 2008), in particular 17–22.

12. G. Bataille, "Le surréalisme et sa différence avec l'existentialisme," in *Oeuvres complètes*, bk. 11 (Paris: Gallimard, 1970–88), 79–80.

13. Ibid., 81.

14. Ibid., 314.

15. Ibid., 312.

16. G. Bataille, "Les problèmes du surréalisme," in *Oeuvres complètes*, bk. 7, 454.

17. Ibid., 314.

18. Ibid., 456.

19. G. Bataille, "Le surréalisme en 1947," in *Oeuvres complètes*, bk. 11, 260.

20. H. Rosenberg, *The De-Definition of Art* (Chicago: University of Chicago Press, 1983), 100–101.

21. http://homepages.neiu.edu/~wbsieger/Art201/201Read/201-Pollock.pdf.

22. Ibid., 3.

23. C. Harrison, "Abstract Expressionism," in *Concepts of Modern Art*, ed N. Stangos (London: Thames & Hudson, 2006),[4] 179. See also I. Sandler, *The Triumph of American Painting. A History of Abstract Expressionism* (New York: Hagertown/Harper & Row, 1970). For an interesting overview that also looks at the meaning of Surrealism in the United States, see F. Tedeschi, *La Scuola di New York* (Milano: Vita e Pensiero, 2004), endowed with an exhaustive bibliography.

24. Harrison, "*Abstract Expressionism*," 186.

25. Rosenberg, *The De-Definition of Art*, 101.

26. Ibid., 106.

27. Ibid.

28. Ibid., 107.

29. B. Newman, "The Ideographic Picture," in *Art in Theory 1900–1990: An Anthology of Changing Ideas*, ed. C. Harrison and P. Wood (Oxford: Blackwell, 1999), 566.

30. Newman, "The Sublime is Now," in *Art in Theory*, 572.

31. Ibid., 573.

32. Ibid., 574.

33. See Rosenberg, *The De-definition of Art*, 100–107.

34. The attention was brought to this by E. Auerbach, "The Aesthetic Dignity of the 'Fleurs du mal,'" in *Scenes from the Drama of European Literature* (Minneapolis: University of Minnesota Press, 1984).

35. C. Baudelaire, "The Painter of Modern Life," in *Selected Writings on Art and Literature* (London: Penguin, 1972), 402.

36. A. Boatto, *Pop Art in USA* (Milano: Lerici, 1967), 20–21.

37. Ibid., 25.

38. Ibid., 27.

39. In this respect, see A. Danto, "The Philosopher as Andy Warhol," in *Philosophizing Art. Selected Essays,* (Los Angeles: University of California Press, 1999), 61–83.

40. A. Warhol, *The Philosophy of Andy Warhol* (Orlando: Harvest, 1977), 15.

41. Ibid., 64.

42. Ibid., 66.

43. Ibid., 71.

44. Ibid.
45. Ibid.
46. Ibid.

Conclusion. Classicism, Again

1. T. Adorno and M. Horkheimer, *Dialectic of Enlightenment* (London: Verso, 1997).

2. As evidenced not only by the romantic tradition and authors such as Paul Valery, but also by some of the most recent developments of the theory of evolution oriented toward evolutionary developmental biology (evo–devo): see in this regard S.B. Carroll, *Endless Forms Most Beautiful. The New Science of Evo Devo and the Making of the Animal Kingdom* (New York: W.W. Norton & Company, 2005).

3. I. Kant, *Critique of the Power of Judgment* (Cambridge: Cambridge University Press, 2002).

4. In this context one should also reconsider the ways of symbolic signification; see E. Franzini, *I simboli e l'invisibile. Figure e forme del pensiero simbolico* (Milano: Il Saggiatore, 2008).

5. See in this regard A. Dal Lago and S. Giordano, *Mercanti d'aura* (Bologna: Il Mulino, 2006).

6. M. Augé, *Non-places: Introduction to an Anthropology of Supermodernity* (London: Verso, 2009).

7. See my "Sulla storia del circolo ermeneutica dal Romanticismo a Gadamer," in *Ciò che l'autore non sa* (Milano: Guerini, 1988), 35–53, in particular 46ff.

8. In this regard, allow me to mention my "Forma come comunicazione: Da Goethe a Carus," in *Annuario Filosofico* (2007): 223–32.

9. M. Heidegger, *Martin Heidegger: Philosophical and Political Writings*, ed. M. Stassen (London: Continuum, 2003), 265ff.

10. J.W. Goethe, *Maxims and Reflections* (London: Penguin, 2005).

11. E. Morin, *La methode 3. La connaissance de la connaissance* (Paris: Editions du Seuil, 1986).

12. G. Rizzolati and C. Sinigaglia, *So quel che fai. Il cervello che agisce e i neuroni a specchio* (Milano: Cortina, 2006); M. Jacoboni, *I neuroni a specchio. Come capiamo ciò che fanno gli altri* (Torino: Bollati Boringhieri, 2008).

13. S. Zeki, *Inner Vision: An Exploration of Art and the Brain* (Oxford: Oxford University Press, 1999), 47.

Bibliography

Adorno, T. *Aesthetic Theory*. London: Continuum, 1997.

———. *The Jargon of Authenticity*. Evanston, IL: Northwestern University Press, 1973.

———. *Negative Dialectics*. Translated by Dennis Redmond. 2001. http://monkeybear .info/ND_Full.pdf.

Adorno, T., and M. Horkheimer. *Dialectic of Enlightenment*. London: Verso, 1997.

Alquié, F. *Philosophie du surréalism*. Paris: Flammarion, 1955.

Aristotle. *Poetics*. New York: Penguin Classics, 1996.

Arnheim, R. *Entropy and Art*. Berkeley: University of California Press, 1971.

Auerbach, E. "The Aesthetic Dignity of the Fleurs du mal." In *Scenes from the Drama of European Literature*. Minneapolis: University of Minnesota Press, 1984.

Augé, M. *Non-places: Introduction to an Anthropology of Supermodernity*. London: Verso, 2009.

Bataille, G. *Oeuvres completes*. Paris: Gallimard, 1970–88.

Baudelaire, C. "The Painter of Modern Life." In *Selected Writings on Art and Literature*. London: Penguin, 1972.

Bäumler, A. "Hellas und Germanien (1937)." In *Studien zur deutschen Geistesgeschichte*. Berlin: Junker und Dünnhaupt, 1943.

Béguin, A. *L'âme romantique et le rêve, essai sur le romantisme allemand et la poésie française*. Marseille: Cahiers du Sud, 1937.

Behler, E. *Unendliche Perfektibilität. Europäische Romantik und Französische Revolution*. Paderborn: Schöningh, 1989.

Beierwaltes, W. *Platonismus und Idealismus*. Frankfurt: Klostermann, 1972.

Beiser, F.C. *The Early Political Writings of The German Romantics*. Cambridge, MA: Cambridge University Press, 1966.

Bellan, A., L. Cortella, and M. Ruggenini. *Adorno e Heidegger. Soggettività, arte, esistenza*. Roma: Donzelli, 2005.

Belting, H. *Das unsichtbare Meisterwerk*. München: Beck, 1998.

———. *Die Deutschen und ihre Kunst*. Munich: Beck, 1992.

Bendavid, L. "Ueber griechische und gothische Baukunst." In *Die Horen. Eine Monatsschrift* 3 (1795) 8:87–102. Reprinted Darmstadt: Wissenschftliche

Buchgesellschaft, 1959. http://www.ub.uni- bielefeld.de/diglib/aufkl/horen /horen.htm.

Benjamin, W. *The Arcades Project.* Cambridge, MA: Harvard University Press, 2002.

———. *Illuminations.* New York: Houghton Mifflin Harcourt, 1968.

Beßlich, B. *Faszination des Verfalls: Thomas Mann und Oswald Spengler.* Berlin: Akademie Verlag, 2002.

Bloch, E. *The Spirit of Utopia.* Stanford, CA: Stanford University Press, 2000.

Blumenberg, H. *Die Lesbarkeit der Welt.* Frankfurt: Suhrkamp, 1979.

———. *Work on Myth* (1979). Cambridge: MIT Press, 1988.

Boatto, A. *Pop Art in USA.* Milano: Lerici, 1967.

Bodei, R. *Le forme del bello.* Bologna: Il Mulino, 1995.

Boehm, G., ed. *Beschreibungskunst—Kunstbeschreibung: Ekphrasis von der Antike bis zur Gegenwart.* München: Fink, 1995.

Bohrer, K.H. "Il fantastico romantico come coscienza decentrata." In *Romanticismo e Modernità*, edited by C. Ciancio and F. Vercellone, 119–41. Turin: Zamorani, 1996.

Bollnow, O.F. "Was heisst, einen Schriftsteller besser verstehen, als er sich selber verstanden hat?" In *Das Verstehen. Drei Aufsätze zur Theorie der Geisteswissenschaften.* Mainz: Kirckheim & Co., 1949.

Breidbach, O., and E. Haeckel. *Bildwelten der Natur.* München: Prestel, 2006.

Breidbach, O., M. Di Bartolo, and F. Vercellone. "La seppia e il sublime. Note sulla naturalizzazione dell'estetica contemporanea." In *Estetica* 2 (2004): 5–32.

Broch, H. "Kitsch" (1933) and "Notes on the Problem of Kitsch" (1950). In *Kitsch: The World of Bad Taste*, edited by G. Dorfles. New York: Bell Publishing, 1969.

Bürger, P. *Theorie der Avantgarde.* Frankfurt: Suhrkamp, 1974.

———. *Theory of the Avant-Garde.* Manchester: Manchester University Press, 1984.

———. *Theory of the Avant-Garde.* Minneapolis: University of Minnesota Press, 1984.

Carchia, G. *Arte e bellezza. Saggio sull'estetica della pittura.* Bologna: Il Mulino, 1995.

———. *L'estetica antica.* Roma-Bari: Laterza, 1999.

Carroll, S.B. *Endless Forms Most Beautiful. The New Science of Evo Devo and the Making of the Animal Kingdom.* New York: W.W. Norton & Company, 2005.

Cheng, F. *Cinq méditations sur la beauté.* Paris: Albin Michel, 2006.

Clair, J. *Considérations sur l'État des Beaux-Arts. Critique de la modernité.* Paris: Gallimard, 1983.

Cometa, M. *L'età di Goethe.* Roma: Carocci, 2006.

Condorcet, J. "Esquisse d'un tableau historique des progrès de l'esprit humain. Ouvrage posthume de Condorcet [1795]." First published in *Philosophisches Journal einer Gesellschaft teutscher Gelehrten* 3: 2 (1795): 161–72.

Cortella, L., M. Ruggenini, and A. Bellan, eds. *Adorno e Heidegger. Soggettività, arte, esistenza.* Roma: Donzelli, 2005.

Croce, B. *Aesthetic As Science Of Expression And General Linguistic.* London: Macmillan & Co., 1909.

————. *La poesia*. Roma-Bari: Laterza, 1953.[5]

D'Angelo, P. *Estetismo*. Bologna: Il Mulino, 2003.

Dal Lago, S. and S. Giordano. *Mercanti d'aura*. Bologna: Il Mulino, 2006.

Danto, A. *The Abuse of Beauty: Aesthetics and the Concept of Art*. Chicago: Open Court, 2003.

————. *Beyond the Brillo Box. The Visual Arts in Post-historical Perspective*. Los Angeles: University of California Press, 1992.

————. "The Philosopher as Andy Warhol." In *Philosophizing Art. Selected Essays*. Los Angeles: University of California Press, 1999.

————. *Philosophizing Art. Selected Essays*. Los Angeles: University of California Press, 1999.

Demandt, A., and J. Farrunkopf, eds. *Der Fall Spenglers. Eine kritische Bilanz*. Köln: Böhlau, 1994.

Derrida, J. *The Truth in Painting*. Chicago: Chicago University Press, 1987.

Dilthey, W. "Construction of the Historical World." In *Dilthey: Selected Writings*. Cambridge, MA: Cambridge University Press, 1976.

————. *Gesammelte Schriften*. Vol. 5, *Die geistige Welt. Einleitung in die Philosophie des Lebens, erste Hälfte, Abhandlungen zur Grundlegung der Geistewissenschaften* (Stuttgart: Vandenhoeck and Ruprecht, 1957).

Dorfles, G., ed. *Kitsch: The World of Bad Taste*. New York: Bell Publishing, 1969.

Duque, F. *Abitare la terra. Ambiente, umanismo, città*. Bergamo: Moretti & Vitali, 2007.

Eco, U. *Arte e bellezza nell'estetica medieval*. Milano: Bompiani, 1987.

Filoni, M. *Il filosofo della domenica. La vita e il pensiero di Alexandre Kojève*. Torino: Bollati Boringhieri, 2008.

Frank, M. "'Ogni verità è relativa, ogni sapere simbolico.' Motivi dello scetticismo nei confronti del principio fondamentale nel primo romanticismo jenese (1796)." In *Romanticismo e modernità*, edited by J. Ciancio and F. Vercellone, 47–74. Turin: Zamorani, 1996.

————. "Philosophische Grundlagen der Frühromantik." In *Athenäum. Jahrbuch für Romantik*. Vol. 4, Paderborn: Schoeningh, 1994.

Franzini, E. *L'estetica del Settecento*. Bologna: Il Mulino, 1995.

————. *I simboli e l'invisibile. Figure e forme del pensiero simbolico*. Milano: Il Saggiatore, 2008.

Franzini, E., M. Ferraris, T. Griffero, and F. Vercellone, eds. *Ciò che l'autore non sa: ermeneutica, tradizione, critica*. Milano: Guerini e Associati, 1988.

Frigo, G.F., ed. *Bios e anthropos. Filosofia, biologia e antropologia*. Milano: Guerini, 2007.

Fuhrmans, M. *Schellings Philosophie der Weltalter: Schellings Philosophie in den Jahren 1806–1821. Zum Problem des Schellingschen Theismus*. Düsseldorf: Schwann, 1954.

Fumagalli Beonio Brocchieri, M. *L'estetica medieval.* Bologna: Il Mulino, 2002.

Gadamer, H.G. *Truth and Method.* London: Bloomsbury Academic, 2004.

Gentili, C., W. Stegmaier, and A. Venturelli, eds. *Metafisica e nichilismo. Löwith e Heidegger interpreti di Nietzsche.* Bologna: Pendragon, 2006.

Gilodi, R. *Una vita in forma di libro. Ermeneutica e romanzo tra Illuminismo e Romanticismo.* Genova: Il Melangolo, 2005.

Givone, S. *Il bibliotecario di Leibniz. Filosofia e romanzo.* Torino: Einaudi, 2005.

Goethe, J.W. "Die Absicht Eingeleitet" [1807]. In *Zur Morphologie* 1:1. Collected in *Goethe. Die Schriften zure Naturwissenschaft,* 1st division, vol. 9, edited by Dorothea Kuhn. Weimar: Bohlaus Nachfolger 1954.

———. *"Betrachtung* über *Morphologie* überhaupt."In Werke, Kommentare und Register. Hamburger Ausgabe in 14 Bänden, Band 13, 5th ed. Hamburg: Wegner, 1966.

———. "Einwirkung Der Neueren Philosophie." *Erstdruck: Zur Morphologie* I:2 (1820).

———. *Goethe's Literary Essays.* Edited by J.E.. Spingarn. New York: Harcourt, Brace and Company, 1921.

———. *Maxims and Reflections.* London: Penguin, 2005.

———.*Studie nach Spinoza, 7–8.*

Gräf, H.G., and A. Leitzmann, eds. *Der Briefwechsel zwischen Schiller und Goethe nach den Handschriften des Goethe- und Schiller-Archivs.* 3 vols. Leipzig: Insel, 1965.

Grassi, E. *Arte come antiarte. Saggio sulla teoria del bello nel mondo antico.* Torino: Paravia, 1972.

Guyer, P. *Values of Beauty: Historical Essay in Aesthetics.* Cambridge, MA: Cambridge University Press, 2005.

Haeckel, E. *Generelle Morphologie der Organismen.* 2 vols. Berlin: Reimer, 1866. Reprinted Berlin: de Gruyter, 1988.

———. *Kunstformen der Natur* (1904). *Die einhundert Tafeln.* With a commentary by R.P. Hartmann and contributions by O. Breidbach and I. Eibl-Eibesfeldt. München: Prestel, 1998.

Harrison, C. "Abstract Expressionism." In *Concepts of Modern Art,* edited by N. Stangos, 179. London: Thames & Hudson, 2006.

Hegel, G.W.F. *Aesthetics. Lectures on Fine Art.* Translated by T.M. Knox. 2 vols. Oxford: Clarendon Press, 1975.

Heidegger, M. "European Nihilism." In *Nietzsche, IV: Nihilism,* edited by D.F. Krell, 8. New York: Harper & Row, 1982.

———. *Martin Heidegger: Philosophical and Political Writings,* edited by M. Stassen, 265ff. London: Continuum, 2003.

———. *Off the Beaten Track.* Cambridge, MA: Cambridge University Press, 2002.

———. "Uber 'die Linie.'" In *Zur Seinsfrage.* Frankfurt am Main: Klostermann, 1959.

————. "Zu Ernst Jünger." In *Gesamtausgabe*, edited by P. Trawny, vol. 4, band 90, 365. Frankfurt am Main: Klostermann, 2004.

Herder, J.G. "Von deutscher Art und Kunst." In *Schriften zur Ästhetik und Literatur 1767–1781*, edited by G.E. Grimm, 443–562. Frankfurt am Main: Deutscher Klassiker Verlag, 1993.

Herf, J. *Il modernismo reazionario. Tecnologia, cultura e politica nella Germania di Weimar e del terzo Reich.* Bologna: Il Mulino, 1988.

Hesiod. *Theogony.* London: William Heinemann, 1914.

Hülsewig-Johnen, J., ed. *Der Blaue Reiter. Avantgarde und Volkskunst. Sammlung Hertha Koenig.* Bielefeld: Medien, 2003.

Jacoboni, M. *I neuroni a specchio. Come capiamo ciò che fanno gli altri.* Torino: Bollati Boringhieri, 2008.

Jauss, H.R., ed. *Die nicht mehr schöne Kunste: Grenzphänomene des* Ästhetischen. München: Fink, 1968.

Jünger, E. Über *die Linie.* Frankfurt am Main: Klostermann, 1952.

Kandinsky, W. "On the Question of Form." In *Theories of Modern Art: A Source Book by Artists and Critics*, edited by H.B. Chipp, P. Selz, and J.C. Taylor, 155. Berkeley: University of California Press, 1968.

Kandinski, W., and F. Marc, eds. *The Blaue Reiter Almanac.* New Documentary Edition. London: Thames and Hudson, 1974.

Kant, I. *Critique of the Power of Judgment.* Cambridge, MA: Cambridge University Press, 2002.

Klee, P. *Paul Klee Notebooks.* Vol. 1. Edited by J. Spiller. London: Lund Humphries, 1961.

Krämer, H. *Il paradigma romantico nell'interpretazione di Platone.* Napoli: Istituto Suor Orsola Benincasa, 1991.

————. *Plato and the Foundations of Metaphysics: A Work on the Theory of the Principles and Unwritten Doctrines of Plato with a Collection of the Fundamental Documents.* New York: SUNY Press, 1990.

Lombardo, G. *L'estetica antica.* Bologna: Il Mulino, 2002.

Luisetti, F., and G. Maragliano, eds. *Dopo il museo.* Turin: Trauben, 2006.

Lukács, G. *The Theory of the Novel.* London: Merlin Press, 1963.

Macke, A., and F. Marc. *Il nostro sogno. Lettere 1910–1914*, edited by M. Passaro, 21–30. Milano: Mimesis, 2006.

Mann, T. *Reflections of a Non-Political Man.* New York: Frederick Ungar, 1983.

Marinetti, F.T. "The Founding and Manifesto of Futurism." First published in *Le Figaro*, 20 February 1909. In *Documents of 20th Century Art: Futurist Manifestos*, edited by U. Apollonio, 19–24. Translated by R. Brain, R.W. Flint, J.C. Higgitt, and C. Tisdall. New York: Viking Press, 1973.

Marquard, O. *Aesthetica und Anaesthetica.* München: Fink, 2003.

Masini, F. *Il travaglio del disumano. Per una fenomenologia del nichilismo.* Napoli: Bibliopolis, 1982.

———. *Lo scriba del caos. Interpretazione di Nietzsche.* Bologna: Il Mulino, 1978.

Matteucci, G. "L'esperienza estetica in Wilhelm Dilthey." Introduction to W. Dilthey, *Estetica e Poetica.* Milano: Angeli, 1992.

Middleton, C., ed. *Selected Letters of Friedrich Nietzsche.* Indianapolis, IN: Hackett, 1996.

Mohler, A. *Die konservative Revolution in Deutschland 1918–1932.* 3rd ed. Darmstadt: Wissenschaftliche Buchgesellschaft, 1989.

Moltmann, J. *The Trinity and the Kingdom of God.* Minneapolis, MI: Fortress Press, 1993.

Mörchen, H. *Adorno und Heidegger. Untersuchung einer philosophischen Kommunikationsweigerung.* Stuttgart: Klett-Cotta, 1981.

———. *Macht und Herrschaft im Denken von Heidegger und Adorno.* Stuttgart: Klett-Cotta, 1980.

Morin, E. *La methode 3. La connaissance de la connaissance.* Paris: Editions du Seuil, 1986.

Morris, W. *Architecture, Industry and Wealth.* London: Longmans Press, 1902.

Nacci, M. *Tecnica e cultura della crisi 1914–1939.* Torino: Loescher, 1982.

Negri, A. "Hölderlin, Nietzsche e la 'Histoire.'" In *Giornale critico della filosofia italiana* 44 (1965): 198-229.

Nehamas, A. *Only a Promise of Happiness. The Place of Beauty in a World of Art.* Princeton, NJ: Princeton University Press, 2007.

Niethammer, F.I. *Philosophisches Journal einer Gesellschaft teutscher Gelehrten.* Charleston, SC: Nabu Press, 2012.

Neitzsche, F. *The Antichrist.* New York: Alfred A. Knopf, 1918.

———. "Aus meimem Leben" (1863). In *Werke in drei Bänden.* Vol. 3. München: Karl Hanser Verlag, 1954.

———. *The Complete Works of Friedrich Nietzsche.* Stanford, CA: Stanford University Press, 1995.

———. *The Gay Science.* Leipzig: E.W. Fritzsch, 1887.

———. "A Letter to My Friend in Which I Recommend that He Read My Favorite Poet (19 October 1861)." In *Selected Letters of Friedrich Nietzsche*, edited by C. Middleton, 4. Cambridge: Hackett, 1996.

———. *The Will to Power (Notes written 1883–1888)*, bk. 4, no. 1066. Translated by W. Kaufmann and R. Hollingdale and edited by W. Kaufmann. New York: Vintage Books, 1968.

Newman, B. "The Ideographic Picture." In *Art in Theory 1900–1990: An Anthology of Changing Ideas*, edited by C. Harrison and P. Wood, 566. Oxford: Blackwell, 1999.

———. "The Ides of Art, Six Opinions on What Is Sublime in Art?" *Tiger's Eye* 6 (15 December 1948): 52–53.

Ovid, *Metamorphosis* 6: vv, 1145.

Plato, *Plato in Twelve Volumes*. Vol. 9. Cambridge, MA: Harvard University Press, 1925.

Riout, D. *Qu'est-ce que l'art modern?* Paris: Gallimard, 2000.

Rizzolati, G., and C. Sinigaglia. *So quel che fai. Il cervello che agisce e i neuroni a specchio*. Milano: Cortina, 2006.

Rodi, F. *Morphologie und Hermeneutik. Zur Methode von Diltheys* Ästhetik. Stuttgart: Kohlhammer, 1969.

Rosenberg, H. *The De-Definition of Art*. Chicago: University of Chicago Press, 1983.

Rosenkranz, K. *Aesthetics of Ugliness*. London: Bloomsbury, 2015.

Runge, P.O. *Farbenkugel*. Hamburg: Bey Friedrich Perthes, 1810.

Ruskin, J. *The Stones of Venice*. Edited by J.G. Links. New York: Da Capo, 1960.

Sandler, I. *The Triumph of American Painting. A History of Abstract Expressionism*. New York: Hagertown/Harper & Row, 1970.

Santayana, G. *The Sense of Beauty. Being the Outlines of Aesthetic Theory*. New York: Charles Scribner's Sons, 1896.

Sartwell, C. *Six Names of Beauty*. London: Routledge, 2004.

Schelling, F.W.J. "Timaeus." In *Epoché: A Journal for the History of Philosophy* 12: 2 (Spring 2008): 205–48.

Schlegel, F. *Kritische Friedrich-Schlegel-Ausgabe*. 22 vols. Vol. 18. Edited by by E. Behler in collaboration with J.-J. Anstett and H. Eichner. München: Schöningh/ Thomas, 1962–2006.

———. "Lyceum Fragments." In *Lucinde and the Fragments*. Minneapolis: University of Minnesota Press, 1971.

———. "On Incomprehensibility." In *F. Schlegel's Lucinde and the Fragments*. Minneapolis: University of Minnesota Press, 1971.

———. *On the Study of Greek Poetry*. New York: SUNY Press, 2001.

Schröter, M. *Der Streit um Spengler. Kritik seiner Kritiker*. München: Beck, 1922.

Sedlmayr, H. *Verlust der Mitte: die bildenden Kunst des 19. und 20. Jahrhunderts als Symptom und Symbol der Zeit*. Salzburg: Müller, 1948.

Selz, P. *German Expressionist Painting*. Berkeley: University of California Press, 1974.

Seubold, G. *Das Ende der Kunst und der Paradigmenwechsel in der* Ästhetik. *Philosophische Untersuchungen zu Adorno, Heidegger und Gehlen in systematischer Absicht*. Freiburg-München: Alber, 1997.

Sieferle, R.P. *Die konservative Revolution. Fünf biographische Skizzen*. Edited by P. Lensch, W. Sombart, O. Spengler, E. Jünger, and H. Freyer. Frankfurt am Main: Fischer, 1995.

Sørensen, B.A. *Symbol und Symbolismus in den* ästhetischen *Theorien des 18. Jahrhunderts und der deutschen Romantik*. Copenhagen: Munskgaard, 1963.

Spengler, O. *The Decline of the West*. New York: Albert Knopf, 1926.

———. *Reden und Aufsätze*. München: Beck, 1937.

Steinbach, M., and S. Gerber, eds. *Klassische Universität und akademische Provinz. Die Universität Jena des 19. Jahrhundert bis in die 30er Jahre des 20. Jahrhunderts.* Jena: Bussert & Stadeler Verlag, 2004.

Steiner, W. *Venus in Exile: The Rejection of Beauty in Twentieth Century Art.* New York: Free Press, 2001.

Szondi, P. *Poetica e filosofia della storia.* Edited by R. Gilodi and F. Vercellone. Torino: Einaudi, 2001.

Tatarkiewicz, W. *Ancient Aesthetics.* Reprint. Berlin: Mouton De Gruyter 1970.

———. "Beauty: History of the Concept." In *A History of Six Ideas. An Essay in Aesthetics*, 121–52. New York: Springer, 1980.

———. *Medieval Aesthetics.* Berlin: Mouton De Gruyter, 1971.

Taubes, J. *Vom Kult zur Kultur.* München: Fink, 1996.

Tedeschi, F. *La Scuola di New York.* Milano: Vita e Pensiero, 2004.

Tennemann, W.G. *Grundriss der Geschichte der Philosophie.* 12 vols. Leipzig: Barth, 1798–1819.

Tiedemann, D. *Geist der spekulativen Philosophie.* Marburg: Neue Akademische Buchhandlung, 1791–92.

Vattimo, G. *La società trasparente.* Milano: Garzanti, 1989.

Vercellone, F. "Arte e mondo dell'espressione da Goethe al 'Blauer Reiter.'" In *Bios e anthropos. Filosofia, biologia e antropologia*, edited by G.F. Frigo, 33–50. Milano: Guerini, 2007.

———. "Forma come comunicazione: da Goethe a Carus." In *Annuario filosofico* (2007): 223–32.

———. *Introduzione al nichilismo.* Roma-Bari: Laterza, 1992.

———. *Morfologie del moderno. Saggi di ermeneutica dell'immagine.* Genova: Il Melangolo, 2006.

———. *Nature del tempo. Novalis e la forma poetica del romanticismo tedesco.* Milano: Guerini, 1998.

———. "Sulla storia del circolo ermeneutica dal Romanticismo a Gadamer." In *Ciò che l'autore non sa*, 35–53. Milano: Guerini, 1988.

Vigarello, G. *Histoire de la Beauté.* Paris: Seuil, 2004.

Vivarelli, V. "Empedocle e Zarathustra: dissipazione di ricchezza e voluttà del tramonto. Gli echi delle letture hölderliniane in Così parlò Zarathustra." In *La Biblioteca ideale di Nietzsche*, edited by G. Campioni and A. Venturelli, 201–35. Napoli: Guida, 1992.

Wackenroder, W.H. *Confessions and Fantasies.* University Park: Pennsylvania State University, 1971.

Waibel, V.L. "Hölderlin und Nietzsche über Philistertum und wahre Bildung." In *Nietzsche-Forschung. Jahrbuch der Nietzsche-Gesellschaft* 11(2004): 45–62.

Waldberg, P. *Surrealism.* Oxford: Oxford University Press, 1978.

Warhol, A. *The Philosophy of Andy Warhol.* Orlando: Harvest, 1977.

Winckelmann, J.J. *Reflections on the Painting and Sculpture of the Greeks*. London: A. Millar, 1765.

Wölfflin, H. *Principles of Art History: The Problem Of The Development Of Style In Later Art*. New York: Dover Publications, 1950.

Worringer, W. *Fragen und Gegenfragen*. München: Piper, 1956.

———. *Spätgotisches und expressionistisches Formsystem*. München: Piper, 1956.

———. *Zur Frage der gotischen Monumentalität*. München: Piper, 1956.

Zecchi, S. *La bellezza*. Torino: Bollati Boringhieri, 1990.

Zeki, S. *Inner Vision: An Exploration of Art and the Brain*. Oxford: Oxford University Press, 1999.

Zoja, L. *Giustizia e bellezza*. Torino: Bollati Boringhieri, 2007.

Index